LEARN WINNING STRATEGIES TO SUCCEED FINANCIALLY IN LIFE!

POKER STRATEGIES

for a WINNING EDGE *in*

BUSINESS

DEVELOP A POKER MIND-SET IN ALL ASPECTS OF BUSINESS:
INVESTING • NEGOTIATING • RUNNING A BUSINESS
MARKETING PRODUCTS • MANAGING CLIENTELE
DEALING WITH CO-WORKERS

BY AN EXPERT
POKER PLAYER AND
FORMER WALL STREET
ATTORNEY

DAVID
APOSTOLICO

Prometheus Books

59 John Glenn Drive
Amherst, New York 14228-2119

Published 2007 by Prometheus Books

Inquiries should be addressed to
Prometheus Books
59 John Glenn Drive
Amherst, New York 14228–2119
VOICE: 716–691–0133, ext. 210
FAX: 716–691–0137
WWW.PROMETHEUSBOOKS.COM

11 10 09 08 07   5 4 3 2 1

Library of Congress Cataloging-in-Publication Data

Apostolico, David.
    Poker strategies for a winning edge in business / by David Apostolico.
        p. cm.
    ISBN 978–1–59102–552–8
    1. Success in business. 2. Negotiation in business. 3. Strategic planning. 4. Poker.
I. Title.

HF5386.A597 2007
658.4'012—dc22

2007027077

Printed in the United States on acid-free paper

POKER STRATEGIES

for a WINNING EDGE *in*

BUSINESS

CONTENTS

PREFACE

T he first time I mentioned the concept of this book publicly was on a popular radio show devoted to poker. The host of that show, a well-known poker pundit, commented that "Everything is poker." While that may have been a slight exaggeration, the point was clear. Poker analogies can be useful in many and varied aspects of life.

For instance, what separates top poker players from the rest of the pack is their ability to read other players. Reading other players encompasses many things. It means understanding others' tendencies, interests, motivation, desire, and mood from clues they give, and then applying that understanding to their actions. Think of the broad application of that skill. Whether you are seated across from an adversary at the negotiating table or buying a home from a seller, how beneficial would it be to know and understand that person? The motivation for "reading others" may be different in each of these scenarios, but there is no question in my mind that skills learned at the poker table would be useful to each.

The challenge of writing this book was to avoid the temptation to cover all topics and not to stretch the poker analogy too thin. Thus, my editor, Linda Greenspan Regan, and I decided to focus our efforts on applying poker strategies to the business world and to practical financial situations. As a practicing corporate attorney for close to twenty years, I have firsthand experience in many business environments. I have represented clients large and small in matters ranging from sizable mergers and acquisitions to family business disputes. In addition, I have sat on the board of directors of numerous companies and have worked for a large corporation. Couple this experience with over twenty-five years of playing poker in everything from home games to events on the Professional Poker Tour. Having played poker long before I entered the corporate world, I found myself using poker strategies in my corporate life. Now I want to share what I've learned.

The business world can be many things to many people. *Poker Strategies for a Winning Edge in Business* is divided into eight chapters. The first is an introduction and overview of the applicability of poker to business and answers the question: "Why use poker strategies?" The next two chapters deal primarily with investing, although many of the strategies have broader application and are so noted, including a number of tips for advancing in the workplace. Chapters 4 and 5 take an in-depth look at negotiating tactics. Whether you are selling a business or buying a car, I think you'll find these chapters extremely useful. Behind-the-scene strategies, such as managing clients and choosing who should lead the negotiations, are also discussed. Chapter 6 takes poker strategies to the workplace. Whether you are trying to climb the corporate ladder, dealing with co-workers, trying to sell your idea, or running your own business, the chapter should resonate. Finally, the last two chapters are more general and attempt to teach you how to think like a poker player in order to make improvements in your day-to-day business affairs. While still maintaining a business focus, these chapters come the closest to affirming the "Everything is poker" declaration. I have high hopes that many readers, by the time they finish reading this book, will have begun to implement poker strategies not only in business but in many other areas of their lives. May you find pocket aces in your life and play them to their full potential.

David Apostolico

FOREWORD

Way before the poker boom, I used to play some poker. Back then, poker was a rite of passage, an entry into adulthood. The lessons learned were ones of street smarts and savvy. Through the years, those same skills have served me well, whether the setting was high-stakes negotiations in the boardroom or a car dealership. In fact, I have often heard others describe negotiations as a poker game. In my opinion, that analogy is used all too loosely. Not that it isn't true, but many of those who express it don't really understand poker. Poker is a simple game to learn but a rather complex and nuanced one to master.

I first met David Apostolico when he came to work for QVC as legal counsel over eleven years ago. David came with an impressive resume, but that didn't mean much to me. There are many important skills that don't show up on a resume—things like adaptability, insightfulness, confidence, analytical skills, intuitiveness, and, most important, the ability to read other people. Of course, these are the same qualities that make a good poker player. If I'm going to trust someone, I want to witness firsthand what someone's capabilities are. I need to see it to believe it. It didn't take long for me to realize that David had what it took. He negotiated a number of transactions of increasing importance for us.

When I received a preliminary copy of this manuscript, I read it with a mix of anticipation and cynicism. I was curious to see the connection between poker and business articulated. Yet I had heard the analogy so often that I was afraid it would sound hollow. My fears quickly faded as I began to read. As each chapter unfolded, the connection between poker and other disciplines became readily apparent. Things I knew but had never seen on paper came to life. Here I was, reading for the first time a blueprint of all of the valuable lessons poker teaches us.

Then, about halfway through the book, it hit me. I never knew David was doing all of these things when he was negotiating on our behalf. He hid his hand well—the ultimate sign of a good poker player. Now, he has decided to share that information not only with me but with you. So, next time you hear someone make an analogy to poker, give yourself a knowing wink, secure in the knowledge that you have a clear understanding of what that means along with the means to execute it.

Bill Costello has recently retired from QVC, where he held the positions of chief financial officer and chief operating officer of QVC, Inc., as well as the position of president of QVC International. Prior to that, he was president of Best Products, Inc., and a partner in the international accounting firm of KPMG.

ACKNOWLEDGMENTS

My father may have taught me the basics of poker when I was a young boy, but, more important, he impressed upon me throughout my formative years the notion that I could accomplish anything if I worked hard enough. Throughout my father's career, I never knew him to call in late, take a sick day, or not put forth the extra effort he needed to succeed. He may not have always practiced the poker theories espoused in this book, but no one was going to outwork him. He managed to do this while balancing the raising of four children. He coached my Little League baseball team for years, and by the time I graduated from high school, he had rarely missed a sporting event of mine. My father is not a wordsmith, but actions always scream louder than words.

My mother is a voracious reader. She has an uncanny ability to consume a book quickly and can spell a word backward faster than most (including myself) can spell it forward. Her attempt to impress upon all of us the importance of reading was about as necessary as impressing upon an astronaut the need for a spacesuit. When my mother had a spare moment, she had a book in her hand. She took weekly trips to the public library where she would return the prior week's stack (with no page unread) and load up on the coming week's reading. I frequently accompanied her, especially during the summer recess when I did not have access to the school library. I have never known a time when I did not have a backlog of books to read.

There are numerous people who have offered support and advice throughout my poker career, including Antonio Esfandiari, Phil Laak, Andy Bloch, Tom McEvoy, Wade Andrews, Earl Burton, Lou Krieger, and Michael Craig. I may never have advanced, however, were it not for the regular trips to Atlantic City I used to take with my brother-in-law Jim Woods. We would make the ninety-minute drive, play a tournament, and then discuss every hand in detail on the ride back home.

I would like to thank the fabulous trio at Sheree Bykofsky Associates: Sheree Bykofsky, Janet Rosen, and Caroline Woods. They believed in this work, stuck with it, and found a wonderful home for it at Prometheus Books. Linda Greenspan Regan, executive editor at Prometheus, helped greatly in shaping the focus of this book into something very tangible and, hopefully, very practical and useful to the reader. Her insight and guidance was as welcomed as it was beneficial. Working with Prometheus has been a first-rate experience and I would like to thank the entire team including Jonathan Kurtz, Jill Maxick, Mark Hall, Rich Snyder, Joe Gramlich, and Marcia Rogers.

Of course, I owe my biggest debt of gratitude to my full house at home. My wife, Cindy, never wavers in her support of my writing even when my head is hunched over the computer while she looks after three highly energetic young boys. She's also an excellent sounding board for all of my ideas. She has a terrific sense of what works and what doesn't and she'll always give me a straight answer. I greatly value her opinion even if my ego sometimes prevents me from processing that opinion right away. Writing a book eats up a lot of time that could otherwise be spent with my family. My wife and children are the best, and I owe them a lot of my attention now that I'm done. I'm incredibly lucky to have them and I know that I wake up with a royal flush every morning.

1. DRAWING CARDS:
WHY USE POKER STRATEGIES?

E ver since poker proliferated along the Mississippi in the early 1800s, it has been the quintessential American game. Poker, if played correctly, embodies all of the qualities cherished in our society, including ingenuity, hard work, creativity, and perseverance. The ability to read and outwit your opponents, which is so essential to success at the poker table, is equally important in forging ahead in a free market. Healthy competition is the cornerstone to capitalism, and playing poker requires a competitive drive that is both primitive and refined.

A poker player must possess a tenacity and ruthlessness capable of taking every last cent from her opponents. Yet, the poker room is not a jungle. Blind aggression will lead to ruin. The competitive nature must be nurtured and directed. Above all else, poker requires objectivity, patience, and discipline. Good players know when the time is right to attack and when the time is right to lay in wait.

The nature of poker, much like business and life, can be random and chaotic. There are numerous factors both under and outside of your control to evaluate. Poker forces players to be rational, to focus on the aspects that they can control and minimize the impact of those factors outside of their control. Of paramount importance is remembering that nothing worthwhile can be gained at the poker table, or in business, without risk. Successful poker players are adept at evaluating and managing risk. They put their money to work when they perceive an edge and hold onto their chips when they don't.

Poker is not played in a vacuum. To be successful, you have to be completely aware of your environment and how that environment is constantly changing. You can sit at the same poker table all night and play against a number of different opponents. Players come and go, other players stay but change their style of play, and your chip stack may go up or down. Throughout this time, your opponents will be focusing on you and making adjustments. A common mistake of beginning players is to play poker as if it were solitaire. They focus on their own hands in isolation and any attention they give to their opponents is an afterthought. Ignore your environment (and specifically your competition), and the results will be disastrous.

Another common mistake of novices, as well as many more experienced players, is to let recent results affect their game more than it should. A sudden rush of cards can make a player feel invincible. That invincibility will lead to carelessness and an empty wallet. A tough run of cards may have a poker player second-guessing his strategies. He may push his luck, feeling he's due or, alternatively, play scared, neither of which is optimal.

These concepts—adjusting to your environment and not letting recent results affect your game—may appear paradoxical, but they are not. Becoming more aggressive when you sense your opponents are playing overly timid is making a proper adjustment to your environment. Believing that you are due a pot because you haven't won one in a while is letting the situation dictate your behavior. Poker players train themselves to remain detached and objective so they can concentrate on the factors that they can control and not worry about what they cannot.

History is full of successful leaders, from heads of state to CEOs, who were quite proficient at poker. Most famously, perhaps, President Richard M. Nixon reportedly financed his first congressional campaign with monies he won playing poker in the US Navy during World War II. Ironically enough, one of Nixon's worst campaign defeats can be attributed to his having been duped by a classic poker maneuver. Many experts blame Nixon's defeat to John F. Kennedy in the 1960 general election to his performance in the first televised presidential debate in history. In that debate, Kennedy appeared healthy, radiant, and confident while Nixon looked tired and washed-out. What isn't well known is that before the debate both Nixon and Kennedy were in the same dressing room getting prepared. A makeup person approached Kennedy, who declined being made up in a voice loud enough voice for Nixon to hear. When the makeup artist then turned to Nixon, he did not want to appear any less macho than Kennedy, so he declined as well. By taking the first action, Kennedy led Nixon exactly where he wanted him to go, which resulted in Nixon looking much worse on air than Kennedy. For an excellent account of this encounter, see Christopher Matthews's book *Kennedy & Nixon*, page 149.

In David Sklansky's landmark book *The Theory of Poker*, he set out his famous Fundamental Theorem of Poker: "Every time you play a hand differently from the way you would have played it if you could see all your opponents' cards, they gain; and every time you play your hand the same way you would have played it if you could see all their cards, they lose. Conversely, every time opponents play their hands differently from the way they would have if they could see all your cards, you gain; and every time they play their hands the same way they would have played if they could see all your cards, you lose."

In the aforementioned Kennedy-Nixon encounter, Nixon played his hand differently from the way he would have played it if he knew what Kennedy was doing (assuming that Kennedy did, in fact, desire that Nixon decline the makeup). In fact, he most likely played it differently from the way he would have played it if Kennedy were not in the room. Kennedy not only hid his cards but sent a false signal to Nixon that Nixon fell for. Kennedy won the hand and would end up winning the debate and the election.

You don't have to be a good poker player to succeed at business, and not all businesspeople will make good poker players. However, a sound understanding of the principles necessary for success in poker will be helpful for business and other aspects of life. In fact, I believe that most people will find it easier to apply successful poker principles to winning at business than to winning at poker. One common thread among successful businesspersons and poker players is a strong desire to succeed and win. They want in on the game and to take their chances, win or lose.

Poker players often make the assumption that because poker is a game of skill, it's not gambling. While I agree that poker is 100 percent skill in the long run, I disagree that it's not gambling. If you look up the definition of gambling on dictionary.com, you get a few different definitions. The first is "to bet on an uncertain outcome, as of a contest." That seems applicable to poker. Poker is a contest, and the way one wins is by betting on an outcome that in the majority of cases is uncertain. There is nothing in this definition that would refute the notion that the contest (in this case, poker) is not one of skill.

Now, let's move on to the next definition, which is "to play in a game of chance for stakes." When players assert that poker is not gambling, they seem to be trying to distance themselves from this definition. A "game of chance" is different from a "contest." Slots, for instance, are clearly a game of chance. There is nothing a player can do to increase her potential winnings. All she can do is put money in the machine, pull the lever, and hope for the best. Whether she wins or loses is entirely up to chance. While the distinction between these two definitions is admittedly slight, I'll still ask the question: Would you rather have your money working for you in a contest of skill in which the outcome is uncertain or a game of chance based purely on luck?

There is a third definition of gambling, however, that reads "[t]o take a risk in the hope of gaining an advantage or benefit." This is poker. Rather, this is smart poker. Good players commit their chips only when they perceive an advantage. We're still under the definition of gambling, but now we're talking about taking calculated risks when you believe you have a positive expected return. If you're playing slots, you have a negative expected return no matter what you do. The machines are programmed to give the house a significant edge. If we open up this last definition, we can see that it has a much broader application than just to poker or other contests of skill.

When we get up in the morning and go to work, we are taking a chance. If we stay safely indoors all day, our chances of getting in a horrible car accident are certainly less than if we make the commute to work. Arguably, the truly prudent man would never leave his home. Nevertheless, we risk that accident in order to go to our jobs, put in a hard day's work, make some money, and improve our lot in life. The tiny risk weighed against the potential benefit seems well warranted. That's an easy one. Now, suppose you have a safe, secure job that pays enough to live comfortably and without much stress. An opportunity arises to go to a start-up where your potential earnings could go through the roof if the company makes it. If it doesn't, however, you could be out of a job within a couple of years. Weighing that risk/reward ratio becomes more difficult. Some of the questions you would need to consider are, what is the potential upside and how hard will it likely be to find another job in a few years if this doesn't work out? This opportunity should also cause you to evaluate your current position. You might ask yourself if this job is as secure as you believe it to be. Finally, and perhaps most important, you want to ask yourself what you really want to get out of life. Everyone must come to his own level of comfort in balancing risk and reward. A fundamental understanding of poker principles can help you find your own comfort zone.

Lest you think I am advocating taking on more risk in life, let's take a look at one last definition of gambling: "[t]o engage in reckless or hazardous behavior." As I hope I just illustrated, gambling is an essential aspect of almost every decision we make, even if we are not always consciously aware of it. Rather than ignore that concept, it is better to understand and control it. Gambling is a slippery slope. Successful poker players are adept at finding that sweet spot where the expected benefit is maximized. Push it too far, though, be it in cards, business, or life, and you risk crossing the edge into self-destructive behavior.

Before we get started, keep in mind three important details. First, poker success is measured over the long term. Most poker players (at least the successful ones) will view their poker contests as one continuous lifelong game. This attitude allows them to remain objective and emotionally detached from short-term profit and loss swings.

Mike Caro, one of the foremost poker authorities in the world, is known for beginning his poker lectures with the question "What is the objective of playing poker?" Invariably, he gets answers such as "making money," "winning pots," or "beating your opponents." All of these are wrong. To paraphrase Caro, the right answer is to make correct decisions. If you can consistently make the right decisions, then the results will eventually come. While this concept sounds simple, it is rather difficult to pull off for a number of reasons, among them our mood, the environment, and the other players at the table. However, the biggest factor that prevents most of us from making correct decisions is the presence of luck—which is the second detail I want you to keep in mind.

Machiavelli was one of the first philosophers to grapple with luck. He believed that no matter what course of action an individual embarked on, he was sure to encounter problems both random and unknown. Machiavelli even went so far as to quantify the role of luck in one's life. He believed that luck accounted for approximately half of one's successes or failures while the individual was responsible for the other half. I don't know how accurate those numbers are, but anyone who has spent time in a poker room can attest to the large and random role that luck plays. Of course, luck is prevalent in all aspects of our lives. How one deals with it can go a long way in determining success. One shouldn't let good luck disguise a poor decision any more than one should let bad luck undermine a good decision. Play poker long enough and you are forced to be objective and recognize the effect of luck—good and bad. If you don't, you won't be very successful. Luck is sometimes harder to detect in the business world, which is why I want you to keep it in mind. I don't suggest overcompensating and attributing every consequence to luck. While I think Machiavelli's 50/50 ratio is fairly accurate in the poker room, the emphasis on luck is probably too high in business and our everyday lives. Be objective in your recognition. Prepare and plan for luck and don't allow it to disrupt your overall plan.

The last factor to keep in mind concerns deception. Certainly, a huge part of the appeal of poker is the deception involved in the game. No one wants to be thought of as the sucker in poker or business. We want to be the ones deceiving, not the ones duped. Poker offers the perfect arena for us to act out our most cunning desires. Deception is not only accepted but expected. Even in poker, however, there are moral boundaries. Cheating is never acceptable. Some players try borderline tricks such as a fake check (making an inaudible signal such as waving one hand implying a check, which in this context means to pass when it is your turn to bet) when the dealer is not looking to see how their opponents react. Tricks like these are called angleshooting and, in my opinion, clearly cross the ethical line.

In business, the boundaries are tighter. In a typical sale of a business agreement, the seller will make a whole slew of representations concerning all aspects of the business. Lawyers will negotiate the terms of those representations and what disclosures the seller must make as an exception to the representations. If the seller has knowledge of a condition that must be disclosed, then by all means it better disclose that information. If it doesn't, that's not deception. That's fraud and there are serious and justified legal consequences for such actions.

Not to worry, there are still plenty of poker principles that will have direct application to business—even some deceptive ones. The seller of a business does not have to show his hand or reveal how interested he is in selling. Poker is a game of subtleties and finesse. Bluffing, while prevalent, is not nearly as big a factor as poker novices believe it to be.

You do not have to be a poker pro in order to understand the principles analyzed in this book. A modest understanding of the fundamentals of the game, however, will enhance your learning experience so you can apply them to business. Since Texas Hold 'em has become the world's most popular game, I will be using it as a reference for poker analogies. For those unfamiliar with the details, I have included a Poker Primer at the back of the book. In addition, there is a glossary of poker terms. Finally, you will notice that I have included a section called "The Poker Experience" at the end of each chapter. These are personal anecdotes that should bring to life some of the points I've made in the preceding chapter.

THE POKER EXPERIENCE

My First Freeroll

When I was a kid, our family would take a weeklong vacation every summer to the Jersey Shore. We'd play on the beach all day, have dinner, and then go to the boardwalk. We would usually just "pound the boards," as my father termed it. However, each night would have one main event. We would play miniature golf one or two nights, go on the rides one night, have pizza another, and go to the arcade for one or two nights. The last night, we always got fresh fudge and saltwater taffy to take home.

During summer in New Jersey, we could usually count on one night of thunderstorms. When that happened, we stayed in and usually read or watched television. I loved to read, but I could do that at home. We had one week at the shore, and I wanted to make the most of every night.

In the summer of 1971, there was not a lot on television to keep a family of six entertained. I was the youngest of four children and was eight years old that summer. My father must have sensed our potential boredom because he planned something special for the inevitable rainy night that week. He brought out a whole jug of pennies with a few nickels mixed in.

Sure enough, we had a thunderstorm that Thursday night. My father surprised us by breaking out the change jar and announcing that we were going to be playing poker. I was vaguely familiar with the game, but this was the first time I would be playing for real stakes— the coins. My father gave us a quick refresher on the game and then divided the money up between the four kids. We'd deal alternating games of five-card draw and five-card stud. Since it rained all night, we inadvertently ended up playing a freezeout, which means we played until one person had all of the coins. That one person ended up being me. (Coincidentally, 1971 was the year that the first freezeout-style tournament made its debut in the championship event at the World Series of Poker. Puggy Pearson often rightfully gets credit for introducing what has become the most popular form of poker, but perhaps my father deserves a mention.)

Now, I don't remember any specific hands or particular poker moves I made that night. To be honest, I would have to say that my win was 90 percent luck. I choose 90 percent not because I think there was a 10 percent skill factor. My siblings were all very bright and at that point had as much knowledge of the game as I did. I was clearly the most interested in the game, though, and I think that counted for something. All things being equal, I think they would have preferred doing something else with their vacation time.

I loved the game, especially the anticipation of "making a hand." Each card dealt brought an opportunity. If you didn't win a pot, a new hand would be dealt, momentarily bringing with it fresh optimism. What I loved the most, though, was raking in the pot after a winning hand. Having a pile of coins in front of me was exhilarating. For me, this was a lot better than the boardwalk. I got a much bigger rush out of this than I could from any ride. Even when we played miniature golf, my favorite part was going for the free game on the eighteenth hole. I liked to win something.

Now here was the chance to win cold hard cash and it didn't cost me a thing. Our father was giving us the chance at our first freeroll. No entry fee, and the winner got to keep the money won. What could be better than this? It sure beat taking out the trash or raking leaves for my allowance.

Of course, there are not a lot of freerolls in life. There are, however, easier ways than others to make money. There's everything from hard labor to investment returns. The great majority of these ways still require work, patience, and objectivity. As has been said many times before, playing poker professionally is a hard way to make an easy living. That statement could be applied to a lot of other disciplines as well.

If you're reading this book, I would venture to say that there is a 75 percent chance that you have an interest in poker, business, or both. However, I am going to go out on a limb and state with near certainty that you are a person with greater than average ambitions. You like to soak in knowledge that will improve yourself and your lot in life. I'm confident that this book will help you.

2. THE END GAME: INVESTING FOR THE LONG TERM

The first thing any poker player needs is a bankroll. Whether you are a professional player or a recreational one, your bankroll should be composed of funds not needed for anything else. This is important because the chips you bring to the table are your "tools of the trade." They are your instruments for winning. A successful poker player looks at those chips the same way that a building contractor looks at a stack of lumber. The chips are a means to building something. A good player puts those chips to work in order to win more chips. Of course, that cannot be done risk free. If a poker player is thinking about what he can buy with those chips, then he has no chance. Those chips are no longer a means to an end. Rather, this inexperienced player will look at those chips as having value in and of themselves rather than being an instrument of his trade.

Investors must take a long-term view. Money set aside for serious investing should be composed of funds not needed for anything else. Those dollars then become the investor's tools of the trade. They are meant to be put to work to earn a return for the investor. If that investor then takes a loss, he's not thinking about what he could have bought with that money. Conversely, when that investor has made a gain, he's not rushing to cash in as he dreams of some exotic purchase. The fluctuations at the poker table can be dramatic. Experienced players realize that the only way to measure success is over the long term when the capriciousness of lady luck will even out. Investors would be wise to take the same approach.

A LOOK AT EXPECTED VALUE

There is a lot of literature out there that looks at "expected value" as the holy grail of the poker decision-making process. (Expected value is what you can expect to win or lose in the long term by making a certain wager.) This viewpoint leaves no gray area; if you are looking at a positive expected value play, then you make it no matter what. Things are never that simple, however, and there should be no absolutes in poker or investing. To illustrate, let's say that you just sat down at the main event of the World Series of Poker to fulfill a life-long dream. The game is no-limit Texas Hold 'em. You realize that you may never play this event again and you want to make the most of this opportunity. By making the most of your chance, you're going to play to win, not just hang onto your chips as long as possible before being eliminated. You are not at the World Series to rub elbows with some past champions and just get some face time on ESPN. You are there to advance as far as possible and make as much money as you can. To do that, you know you can't play risk free.

The very first hand, you are dealt pocket queens in the big blind. (The big blind is a forced bet by a player when he is seated two seats to the left of the rotating button, a round disc that rotates around the table with each new deal.) The big blind is the last person to act before the flop (the first three community cards dealt). Everyone folds to the small blind (the player one seat to the left of the button who must post a bet equal to that of the big blind) who carelessly lifts up his cards for you to clearly see that he has an ace-king, both of spades. He then pushes his entire stack of $10,000 of chips into the middle. You know that your pair of queens is about a 53.5 percent favorite to win. What do you do? If this was a cash game and you were playing well within your bankroll, you should call every time. Whether you win or lose the hand is irrelevant. Over the course of a lifetime of playing, you will make money by consistently making that decision because you have positive expected value. That's not the case here, though. If you lose this hand, you are eliminated. Why risk everything on what is essentially the flip of a coin? The tournament is just getting started, and there will be plenty of other opportunities to put your chips to work when you are more favored. The example is perhaps easier to understand in the context of investing. If someone gave you 53.5 percent odds to risk everything you own, would you do it? You'll double your net worth more than half the time, but you'll go broke nearly half the time. No reasonable person would take that bet. Even if you were given a 75 percent chance of doubling, the downside is too great.

I'm not suggesting that you ignore expected value. Rather, look at it as one factor to consider instead of the only factor. There are even times that you will knowingly take a play with negative expected value. You may try a bluff in poker that you know is unlikely to work. Yet you don't mind getting caught bluffing because it will set your opponents up to call your big bets later when you are not bluffing. There may also be times when you will need to fight back against overly aggressive opponents in order to slow them down. In these cases, you are not looking to make money off the play at hand, but rather you are attempting to preserve your bankroll overall. In investing terms, this is called hedging.

You diversify your portfolio including some assets that you may expect to decline in value. The reason you do this is if some of your other asscts do go south, then these expected decliners are likely to go up. A portfolio including some tech stocks may be offset with investments in natural gas, gold, and commodities.

Know When to Hold 'em and When to Fold 'em

It's an old cliché but still a cardinal rule in both poker and investing. Know when to hold 'em and when to fold 'em. As simple as this advice sounds, many find it very difficult to follow. The reason is twofold (excuse the pun): pride and greed. These are fundamental attributes of human nature. People do not like to admit mistakes and greed often gets the better of us. Success—at the poker table and in life to a large extent—is directly proportional to our ability to overcome these feelings.

Folding a strong, but losing, hand is the hardest thing to do in poker. You could be playing for an hour and not receive a playable hand. Then all of a sudden you get a really strong hand, but your opponent has you beat. Letting go of that hand is extremely difficult. We get emotionally attached. We feel a sense of entitlement. What we fail to do is to keep the hand in perspective. Three aces are no better than a pair of twos when you are up against a full house. In fact, they are a whole lot worse. We would not have any trouble folding those deuces. The aces, however, are likely to cost us a whole lot of money unless we keep our emotions in check. The ability to recognize when you're beat is a survival skill that will serve one well in investing. Nothing should be viewed in a vacuum. Those three aces cannot be played blindly. You must pay attention to what your opponent is doing and what he may have. Your hand must be considered in relation to the hands your opponents may have.

Similarly, if you are thinking about making an investment, do your homework. An investment decision should not be made in a vacuum. If you are contemplating buying the stock of a company, look at the fundamentals of that company. Then make sure you look at the fundamentals of similar and competing companies. See how the relative value of your targeted stock compares with that of other companies. Then look at how the industry of your targeted company compares with other industries. Then look at how stocks are performing against other investments, such as bonds or real estate. The stock of your company does not trade in a vacuum, so your analysis should be broad-based. When you purchase a stock, what are you hoping for? You are hoping that the stock appreciates in price. It will only appreciate in price if others find it attractive as well. There are a lot of different investment opportunities for people out there so you must consider how attractive the stock is relative to all of the other investment opportunities. It doesn't do you any good to make an investment in an asset that you feel is undervalued if the public at large doesn't share your opinion, for it is likely to remain undervalued or it really isn't undervalued in the first place.

If you are buying real estate, the same analysis holds true. Look at the fundamentals of the property you're thinking about purchasing. Then look at the prices of similar properties. Then consider the value of real estate to other investments taking into account interest rate conditions. For instance, you may love a house on a main street but others may be turned off by that location. The location is never going to change, so try to determine the fair-market value, which may be less than what you are willing to pay, since the majority of people will expect a discount for the location.

A common mistake of both poker players and investors is to hold onto a poker hand or investment because they have invested a lot and they want to at least get their money back. Beginning poker players are notorious for staying in hands until the end because they have some money invested in the pot. What they fail to realize is that the money is no longer theirs. Once bet, that money belongs to the pot. Whoever wins the hand will get the money. If you do not have a realistic chance of making a winning hand, throw it away. Of course, there will be times when it is worth drawing another card when the pot is substantial and there are some cards out there that will improve your hand to become a winning one. However, poker players who consistently draw cards until the end of the hand in the face of overwhelming odds—because they want to get their money back—will be big losers.

In a similar vein, it is never too late to fold a hand. Poker can change quickly. You may be the leader after the flop (the first three community cards dealt) with two pair, but the turn (the fourth community card) may give your opponent a flush (five cards of the same suit) and, in the process, make you a long shot to win. Even if you've been betting heavily (as you should have been) in the beginning rounds, it is now time to let go of your hand.

It is never too late to sell a losing investment. If a stock you bought has depreciated 20 percent and the fundamentals have changed for the worse, sell. Too many investors tell themselves that they will sell as soon as it gets back to their original purchase price. The original purchase price is irrelevant. That 20 percent is gone. It is no longer the investor's money. Any analysis should be based on the current price of the stock and whether it is a good investment at that price and worth holding onto. In today's global economy, things can change fast. If the stock is no longer a good investment, sell. As simple as this sounds, it is a very difficult thing to do. The original purchase price creates a psychological barrier to letting go. Human nature being what it is, people do not like to admit that they made a bad investment. The original purchase price creates a false frame of reference. They want to hold on until they get their money back. However, that money is no more theirs than the money that the poker player has thrown into the pot.

Back in the late '90s, I invested in a company that was supposed to be the next great thing in fiber optics. I knew it was a risky venture when I purchased the stock that was trading around $20 a share. Shortly after I invested, the company sold stock to private investors at a price below that and even offered warrants to those investors at $7 a share. Of course, that made the stock price tumble and it should have sounded alarm signals in my head. I was stubborn, though, and rationalized that this was actually good news and would help out the balance sheet. I made this rationalization during a time when venture capital money flowed freely and any viable company could easily raise cash.

Over the next two years, the stock of this company continued to sink. Each time it drifted lower, I swore I would sell the next time it bounced higher. That is, when it fell to $12, I promised I would sell as soon as it was back to $15. When it hit $8, I put in a sell order at $10. When the stock finally went below $2, I bought more, figuring I would sell it at $5 and make some of my money back. I still own this stock to this day and it is trading at a fraction of one cent. I can't even sell it because the commissions would cost me more than I would realize from the sale. If I had only been able to objectively value the current market price at any step rather than holding onto this silly notion that I could somehow recoup my money, I would have saved myself a lot of money and aggravation.

THE 40/70 RULE

Colin Powell is a champion of what is known as the 40/70 rule. Mr. Powell is clearly a man who leads by example and is not afraid to make tough decisions and stick with them. He is a man of action, not inaction. So, what is the 40/70 rule? Mr. Powell believes that you should not take action until you have enough information that you have a probability of being at least 40 percent correct. However, you should never wait until you have enough information to be 100 percent correct. That leads to paralysis by analysis. The sweet spot for action lies somewhere between a 40 percent and 70 percent probability. This rule of thumb seems absolutely perfect for poker, which is a game of imperfect information. Unless you have the absolute nuts (the nuts being the best possible hand), you are never going to be 100 percent sure of winning a hand. Even if you do have the sure winner, you still won't be 100 percent sure of what your opponent has and how to best get as many chips as you can. Yet, we have all seen these ultraconservative players at the poker table unwilling to commit until they are certain of victory. This is a surefire way to spell defeat. These players will never maximize their return on their strongest hands.

The same thing holds true for investing. If you wait to act until you have absolute certainty that a company is going to be successful, you are never going to reap decent returns. Since investors are always looking forward, the opportunity has usually passed by the time all the good news is out. Often, there is even a sell-off as investors "buy the rumor and sell the news."

Superior returns require investing with some degree of uncertainty. That doesn't mean investing blindly. Rather, you should find your own comfort level somewhere in that 40/70 zone.

Take a moment to reflect on your investment style and ask yourself honestly if you are the type of investor who likes close to 100 percent information before acting. If so, then what can you do to improve your returns? The good news is that if you are this type of person, you probably do a tremendous job gathering as much information as possible on potential investments. Maintain that focus. After all, the goal is still to be as informed as possible. The only change is deciding when you should act with that information. If you are focusing on all the pertinent information, then go with your gut. Learn to react rather than overanalyze. This will help you move into the sweet spot of action. Don't worry about making mistakes. Don't worry about being careless. All that information you are gathering is still being processed and used in the decision-making process. It's just being streamlined now. Of course, this is not to say you should make rash judgments based on no information.

If you still can't get yourself to take action with less information, then ask yourself one last question. No matter what stakes you are investing in, have you ever faced a decision that has larger consequences than the decisions Colin Powell has faced? Once we put decision making into proper perspective, investing should open up and not only be more fun but more profitable.

The 40/70 rule has broader application than just to investing and poker. Strong leaders in all disciplines are people of action, not inaction. Take the time to study those people who are successful where you work, and I'd be willing to bet that in the majority of cases, you are going to find individuals who make hard decisions with less than perfect information.

Do Not Bet More Than You Can Afford to Lose

In poker, as in life, there is no such thing as a sure thing. Even if you feel you are by far the best player at the table, anything can happen. Your skill level is only one factor in determining your success at the poker table. There are many other factors—known and unknown— that will play a part in determining the winners. Your position at the table, the skill level of your opponents, and, of course, luck will have a major impact. Of these, luck is the biggest unknown, and most dangerous, factor. Even a bad player can win in the short term when he is getting good cards.

No one can control, or even anticipate, luck. All anyone knows for sure is that luck is arbitrary and capricious. You can, however, mitigate its potential harm by not jeopardizing more than you can afford. Whether you are playing poker or making an investment, do not bet or invest more than you can afford to lose. Similarly, there is no such thing as a sure investment. The value of stocks, real estate, and bonds can go down just as easily as they go up. Stay diversified. Even if you love where you work and know the company inside out, avoid having all of your money tied up in it. Since your salary, and livelihood, is already tied into the company, be careful not to have too much of your retirement plan in company stock. Anything can happen. There's always the unknown.

Whether you play poker professionally or recreationally, you play to win. In the long run, professionals have to make money or else they better find another profession. Knowing this, a good professional knows that he will have losing sessions along the way. That is the nature of poker. That's why professionals know to pace themselves and not bet too much during any one session. That's why professionals become experts in a number of different poker games. They understand the importance of being diversified. If they have a rough streak in one game, they can switch to another game or take a break in order to avoid losing too much. If they become too proficient in one game, they may have a hard time finding others willing to play with them.

Investors have to take a long-term approach and not panic during the short-term variances that are sure to come. Being diversified and not investing more than you can afford to lose will be critical to maintaining that approach. Even your best investments can go south or top out if they run up in a hurry. A periodic evaluation of all of your investments will help you avoid complacency. In addition, a diversified portfolio can become less diversified if one sector is greatly outperforming others. Take the time to reallocate in order to manage risk and minimize luck.

"Do not bet more than you can afford to lose" is a lesson that is applicable to every aspect of business. Companies must manage growth and not overinvest lest they stretch themselves too thin. Similarly, a manager must be careful not to take on more responsibility than she or her team can handle. It's good to be ambitious, but one must be realistic. Doing an inadequate job because you are overtaxed does not serve either you or your company very well. Invest in yourself, but invest wisely. Don't overburden yourself.

LAY DOWN A STRONG HAND WHEN THE FLOP GOES SOUTH

A strong starting hand does not guarantee a winning hand. Good players know how to get rid of those hands when they realize they are in danger. For example, say a player (let's call her Ms. Smart Play) starts with the ace-king, both of hearts, in Hold 'em. This is a very strong starting hand, and she bets it. Two opponents call (they place an amount of chips into the pot equal to the original bet). The flop brings the following cards: 8-9-10, all of spades. Before it is Ms. Smart Play's turn to act, one of her opponents bets and the other calls. Ms. Smart Play folds (she does not call the bet and throws her hand away), which is the right decision. As strong as her starting hand was, it is now highly likely that Ms. Smart Play is up against better hands. An opponent could easily already have a straight or a flush. Even if he doesn't, it is highly likely that one of the opponents will make a straight or flush. Ms. Smart Play's hand has gone from a very strong starting hand to one that is now not even worth playing. While this example would appear to be rather obvious, it is amazing how many players will continue to bet strong starting hands after the flop has gone south on them. They just refuse to give up on a hand that had so much promise. They cannot recognize that the hand has lost a great deal of its value in light of the cards that followed. At this point, it is not worth wasting any more money on the hand. Fold the hand. You will be dealt a new one momentarily.

When circumstances change, react to them. A common theory of investing is that one should never tolerate more than a 10 percent loss. That is, if you buy a stock and it goes down 10 percent, sell it. Even if you do not know what the problem is, others may, and it is better to get out before the stock goes down further. Now, in today's markets, there are plenty of volatile stocks that can easily go up or down 10 percent when nothing has fundamentally changed about the company. However, the theory still has plenty of merit. You can decide how much of a loss you are willing to tolerate. The larger point is that if things go south, get out. Presumably you buy the stock of a company because you feel it has great potential. It is an ace-king–suited starting hand (a hand with an ace and a king of the same suit). The company has a strong and experienced management team, great financial statements, and a strong pipeline of new products coming out. If during the six months following your investment the chief executive officer retires, the SEC (US Securities and Exchange Commission) begins an investigation into the company's accounting practices, and a number of the new product offerings have been delayed due to manufacturing problems, it is safe to say that the flop has gone south on this company. Dump the stock. It no longer holds the promise it did when you bought it. While it is great to be optimistic, you have to be realistic. Potential is only that—it may or it may not amount to anything. Monitor your investments. Treat them as you would a hand of poker. Each bit of news is a new card that is turned over that may or may not help your hand. When you can recognize that an investment is not going to live up to its potential, it is time to move on. Dump the stock and look for a better place to put your money.

ANYTHING CAN HAPPEN

As anyone who has played poker can attest, anything can happen at the poker table. You can do everything right in a hand and still lose. Conversely, you can make big mistakes and win. That's poker. It's not fair, but everyone realizes that there is an inherent risk in every hand. The good player takes calculated risks and lives with the consequences, knowing that if he plays his game, he will win in the long run.

What is so transparent in poker is not so obvious in the business world. We are reminded again and again at the poker table that anything can happen. When the unexpected happens, it happens immediately and is known by all. For example, you get all of your chips in the pot when you are heads-up against an opponent (meaning it is just you and one other opponent left in the hand). You have a full house and your opponent has three jacks. There is one card to come and the only card that can save your opponent is the fourth jack. You are an overwhelming favorite. Lo and behold, that fourth jack comes. Anything has happened. The consequences are felt immediately as you watch the dealer push the large stack of chips in your opponent's direction.

We do not and cannot know the future. We may think an investment in a blue chip company is a safe bet. (A blue chip company is a long-standing publicly traded company with a big market capitalization and a stock price that does not fluctuate greatly.) We make the investment and forget about it. Five years later, the stock has lost 90 percent of its value, since the company has not kept up with key developments in the industry. We ask ourselves how this could have happened. We never saw that fourth jack being dealt. Instead, the company slowly deteriorated in an ever-changing world. What was cutting-edge technology is now virtually obsolete.

The problem is that we did not properly evaluate the consequences. Since anything can happen, any investment has some risk. Not recognizing risk is a huge mistake. I have learned that when I have a strong hand, I am more vulnerable than when I have a weak hand. Why? Because when I have a strong hand, I do not always appreciate the danger. When you are too comfortable, you let your guard down and you forget that anything can happen. If you are completely comfortable with all of your investments, you are probably not appreciating the risks. You are also probably not diversified. No one is comfortable with the prospects for every sector. We all have biases. That is why we need to force ourselves to diversify. Be invested in some areas that make you uncomfortable. You never know which sectors will do well and which will not. We cannot know everything, but if we are smart, we will know that we do not know everything. With diversification comes the recognition of risk. With the recognition of risk comes contemplation and analysis that I hope will permeate throughout all of your investments.

Do Not Let Winning Mask Your Sloppy Play

Everyone who has played enough poker has witnessed poor play rewarded. If you play a lot of hands, you will win a fair number of them. Even if you are sure to lose money in the long run, you will enjoy some success along the way. You may even go on a run that fuels your playing for a while. Those short-term successes are what encourage the poor player to keep playing. He can justify his strategy by pointing to the pots he wins rather than the fact that he is losing money overall. In fact, if the poor player is playing every hand, he will most likely win more hands than anyone else at the table due solely to the fact that he is indeed playing every hand. The trouble is that he will lose a lot more hands—and money—than anyone else at the table. It is human nature, however, to remember your wins and forget your losses. This poor player can easily point to the number of pots he has won and make himself feel good about his play.

In a similar way, do not let a few wins in investing mask a fundamental problem with your investment strategy. If you are investing in ten highly risky tech stocks and one or two do well, do not let this cloud your judgment if you're down overall. To allow yourself to feel good about the one or two wins may help stroke your ego but it will wreak havoc on your portfolio.

In poker, the good players try hard to maintain their objectivity when evaluating their play. Furthermore, they are constantly analyzing their play. They do not allow a few wins to mask their sloppy play. They recognize when they have gotten lucky in a hand that does not fit into their overall strategy of disciplined smart play.

Investors should do the same thing. Take the time to periodically evaluate your portfolio on an objective basis. View each investment individually to see if it fits into your overall game plan. Recognize that it is human nature to want to remember the good investments and forget the bad ones. Say you invested in five micro-cap biotech stocks after reading about them on an Internet message board. After six months, four of them are down significantly, while one (let's call it Company Rise) has doubled in price. Overall, you have lost 50 percent of your initial investment. Do not delude yourself. Avoid convincing yourself that you knew Company Rise was the best one in the lot and if only you had invested everything in Company Rise, you would be in great shape. All this does is mask the underlying problem. If you had really done your research and felt strongly about Company Rise, perhaps you would have invested more in that company. However, the fundamental problem here is that you should not be investing money based on recommendations from message boards.

Anyone can get by with sloppy play in the short term, but no one will do so in the long term. In the business world, there is often a time lag between execution and results. Change (positive or negative) implemented today may not show up until six months to a year from now. At the individual level, mistakes you make may not surface for quite some time. Don't let that delude you. If you feel you've done a sloppy job, then acknowledge it and correct it.

CONCENTRATE ON THE PROCESS, NOT THE END RESULT

Sometimes in poker, you can do everything right and still lose. The experienced player (let's call him Mr. Process) knows this. Mr. Process knows that there will be times when he reads his opponent correctly and bets big, knowing he is way ahead of his opponent. When his opponent calls, Mr. Process is happy because he knows the odds greatly favor him. When his opponent draws two hearts on the last two cards to hit a flush, however, Mr. Process is no longer happy. Yet, Mr. Process is not discouraged. He takes a second to evaluate the hand he just played. Once he comes to the conclusion that he played it correctly, he forgets about it and concentrates on the next hand. Mr. Process does not worry about short-term success or failure due to factors outside of his control. He is secure in the knowledge that if he continues to play the right way, he will succeed in the long run.

Any goal worthwhile in life is the result of hard, steady work. If you never compromise your precepts in your pursuit, you will succeed. Do not allow short-term failures due to factors outside of your control affect your overall investment strategy. If you do a lot of research and work and find what you think is a good real estate investment in an area that is just starting to develop, then go ahead and invest. If interest rates unexpectedly rise and depress property values, do not get flustered. Take the time to evaluate your play. Is the property still a good investment? Interest rates will always fluctuate. If the property is still in a growing area and you still feel it is undervalued, then stay the course. You cannot control interest rates. Interest rates will go up and down, but in the long run your property should appreciate as the surrounding area is developed. Concentrate on the process. If you were investing for the long term, a short dip in value makes no difference, since you were not looking to sell quickly anyway.

While you can never control all of the factors affecting your portfolio and there are no guarantees in life, if you develop a good game plan and concentrate on the result, the end result should take care of itself.

DO NOT RISK EVERYTHING IF YOU DO NOT HAVE THE NUTS

In poker, having the "nuts" is having the absolute best hand possible in the situation. According to legend, the term comes from the eighteenth-century Old West. It was common practice for a player to bet his horse and wagon if he was out of cash. To do so, he would place into the pot the nuts that held the wagon wheels in place. Since that player would be stranded if he lost, he knew that he'd better only bet on the best hand, or the nuts.

So what is the nuts? For instance, say you are playing Texas Hold 'em and the board (the five community cards placed in the center of the table) is queen spades-9 spades-5 clubs-4 spades-2 spades. Anyone holding the ace of spades in this situation would have the nuts, since a flush is the best possible hand and the ace of spades would make the highest possible flush. Therefore, if you are holding the ace of spades, you can bet with impunity. You cannot lose. The only question to ask yourself is how to bet in order to get the maximum amount of money out of your opponents. On the other hand, if you held the king of spades, you would have a strong hand but one that is vulnerable. You would not want to risk everything, since you could be beaten by someone holding the ace of spades.

In the great majority of hands, no one will be holding the nuts. That is what makes poker interesting—and analogous to investing. Everyone is vulnerable. It is up to each player to figure out how his hand stacks up to that of his opponent(s). When a player feels that he has the strongest hand, he wants to do everything he can to maximize his profit, yet he still has to be cautious in the event someone has a stronger hand.

Unfortunately, there is no such thing as the "nuts" when it comes to investing. There are no sure things. You must always weigh the strength of your hand against any and all potential liability. No matter how strongly you believe in an investment, do not risk more than you can afford to lose unless you have the nuts. And you will never have the nuts. Something could always go wrong. Natural disasters happen. Government regulations change. Key executives leave. Big customers go elsewhere or go bankrupt. Most performance contracts have "force majeure" clauses. These are clauses that forgive a company's lack of performance for things out of their control, such as war and acts of God. These clauses are standard because things can always go wrong.

This does not mean that you should not ever invest. You cannot worry about every possible thing that can go wrong. Do your research and diversify your investments. Nothing in life that is worthwhile is without risk. Just do not risk everything if you do not have the nuts.

Not risking everything has broader application to the business world at large. Unlike poker, you can never have the nuts in business. You may have a dynamite product or service, but nothing is foolproof. Be confident and be willing to invest in your ideas and be an advocate for your position. However, try not to stake your entire career or job on any one thing.

DO NOT DO THE RAIN DANCE

Why does the Native American "rain dance" work? Because believers keep dancing until it rains. Some poker players take the same attitude. They keep playing hands until they win. If you play every hand, you are guaranteed to win one sooner or later. In fact, you are likely to win a lot of hands. You may even win more hands than anyone else at the table. If you play every hand, you may win two or three out of ten. Those wins will be very expensive. A good player may only play, on average, two hands out of ten. The good player, however, will win a much higher percentage of the hands he plays and find them to be profitable. The weak player, who plays every hand, will find a winning hand as comforting as a rain shower for a parched land. Those wins will be enough to validate his playing style and keep him going.

Do not do the rain dance when it comes to investing. If you throw enough darts at the wall, one is bound to hit the target. The point is not to chase every opportunity at any cost. The key to success is to be discriminating. Pick the best opportunities and play them. Even then you will not find every one a success. However, your success rate will be much higher. If you take every stock tip someone gives you, you are bound to have a success sooner or later. Do not let this validate the style of your playing. It is human nature to rationalize success. When that rain finally comes, be honest with yourself. At what cost did that rain come? If the cost is too high, change your starting hand requirements. Invest in companies that represent strong starting hands.

DO NOT BE LULLED INTO A FALSE SENSE OF SECURITY BY A LARGE STACK

Players with the largest stacks of chips tend to have the most power at the table. These players are operating from a position of strength and have the means to dominate their opponents.

The players holding the large stacks are not invincible, however. Every poker room in the country is littered with players who have blown large stacks. In tournament play especially, many players (even experienced ones) have seen overwhelming chip leads evaporate. That is the nature of poker. Even the largest stack at the table is vulnerable. If a player lets down his guard, there will be a table full of hungry players more than willing to relieve him of his chips.

While there are certainly some things a player may do differently with a large stack (such as taking more calculated risks), he should not abandon the fundamentals of his play. He should continue to observe his opponents and their play and look for situations to exploit. He should not force the action or play looser than he normally would just because he feels he has chips to spare. Finally, and perhaps most important, he should not rest on his laurels.

When it comes to investing, blue chip companies can be thought of as the large stacks of the poker room. Blue chip companies have come to represent large, dependable low-risk investments. As many

investors have found out, though, blue chip companies are not inde-
structible. One need only look at recent examples such as Enron or
WorldCom to find companies that went from blue chip status to bank-
ruptcy before investors learned how much trouble these companies
were really in.

While blue chip companies on average are typically less risky than
small upstart companies, investors should not abandon their fundamental investment strategy. Investors should continue to do their due
diligence and monitor all the developments of the large-cap companies. Investors should not throw too much money into blue chip stocks
thinking they represent a safe haven for their funds. They need to
maintain a fundamentally sound investment strategy and remain diversified.

Do Not Be Afraid of Losing

One of the fundamental principles of poker is that in order to win, you
must be willing to lose. You never know for sure what your opponent
holds or what cards will come off the deck next. All you can do is use
your experience to best calculate the cards your opponent is holding
and the odds you will win and then play accordingly. You cannot
always think of the worst-case scenario. There will be plenty of times
that you will have the best hand, but there will be very few times that
you will have the best hand possible. If you waited to play only the
best possible hands, you would be playing very few hands indeed. And
when you did play, your opponents would know you had a super
strong hand and would fold, leaving your monster hand unprofitable.
In poker, you play smart and disciplined, but you do not play scared.
("Playing scared" means being tentative and more concerned with
avoiding any loss than trying to win.) If you are playing scared, you
are guaranteed to lose. There will be times when you do everything
right but don't win. Good poker players are not discouraged by losses
if they know they played the hands correctly. If they did not play the

hand correctly, then they learn from their experience and correct their play for future hands.

Do not be afraid of failure. You will not be 100 percent successful in everything you do. None of us has a crystal ball. If we were to worry about everything that could go wrong, we would never take any chances at all. No matter what the investment choice, the key is to do your homework and then make smart, disciplined decisions. Be consistent with your research and decisions and over the long term, you will find success. There will be plenty of bumps and bruises along the way. When you suffer a setback, take the time to evaluate your decision. If it was the correct one, then stay the course. If it was a wrong choice, then learn from your mistake, correct it, and go forward.

Be proactive in your business world as well. Don't be afraid to voice your opinion, ask questions, or present ideas out of fear of rejection. If you are worried that others may not embrace your thoughts, you are greatly limiting your ability to succeed. Between staying quiet and speaking up, the greater risk lies in maintaining your silence.

ON THE KEYBOARD OF POKER, ALWAYS KEEP ONE FINGER ON THE ESCAPE KEY

Good poker players are skeptics at the table. They view everyone and everything with a fair amount of suspicion. They do not trust anyone but themselves. This does not mean that they play every hand because they think everyone else is bluffing all of the time. In fact, quite the opposite is true. Winning poker players are critical thinkers. They view every situation objectively, trying to see where the advantage lies. They look for a reason to justify playing and expending chips. Quite simply, if they do not perceive an advantage, they fold. Why play if someone else has the advantage? Why spend money when your opponent has the best of it? Save your chips for another hand when you either have a strong hand or you believe your opponent is weak and you can chase her out. Good players know a new hand is always just a few short minutes away. Even a very strong starting hand can become a troubling one with the deal of one card. That is why good players always have an exit strategy. Inexperienced players have a hard time folding aces even when it is painfully obvious that one of their opponents is likely to have a flush. They just cannot hit that escape key when that beautiful starting hand turns into a losing one.

Be a critical thinker in your everyday life. Watch investment shows and read money magazines to get investment ideas. Keep in mind, though, that those analysts touting a stock typically only tell you the reasons to buy it. It is up to you to determine all the reasons you should not buy it. Look for a reason not to buy it. If after careful deliberation the touted stock does not add up, fold your hand. There are thousands of other stocks to review. Once you do make an investment, the work and research does not stop. Stay abreast of all developments. What may have started out as a very strong investment can go south in a hurry. Keep a finger on the escape key.

Don't just go through the motions at work. Be well read and up to date at your job. Understand why you are doing things and what you can do to improve. Be a critical thinker and experiment with some new ideas. Bounce them off a trusted colleague. Be innovative but flexible. Not every new idea is going to be a winner. If your idea is too problematic, discard it, and move on to a new idea, or back a co-worker's idea that has more merit. But keep those ideas coming! If you first do your research, and your next idea seems possible, remember to speak up.

IT IS NEVER TOO LATE TO GET OUT OF A HAND

You will often hear someone at the poker table say that they are "pot committed" and then call with an obvious losing hand. What that player means is that he has already put so much money into the pot that he has to call now, even if it costs him two more bets. That player just cannot let go and is trying to rationalize his bad play. Good players know how to make good laydowns—they know that it is never too late to get out of a hand. They realize that once those chips are thrown into the pot, those chips no longer belong to them. The chips now belong to the winning hand. If you do not have a realistic chance of winning the hand, cut your losses and fold. Do not throw good money after bad.

How many times during the stock market crash that lasted from 2000 to 2002 did you hear the popular refrain "Well, it's too late to sell now"? Stocks would drop 20 percent and analysts would come on television and say that it was too late to sell. Then stocks would drop another 20 percent and you would hear the same thing. Then another 10 percent drop. And another. By the time the carnage ended, many stocks were down 90 percent or more. Yet, the whole time down, you heard the refrain that it was too late to sell. This was a popular sentiment that many bought into. Investors were highly emotional. They wanted to get their money back. They were "pot committed." What they failed to realize was that the money was no longer there. It evaporated with the stock price. They had no chance of making that money back, yet they refused to fold their hand. If they had taken the time to reevaluate the situation with the new price and outlook, they could have saved a lot of money. Just as it is never too late to fold, it is never too late to sell.

THE MATHEMATICALLY CORRECT PLAY IS NOT ALWAYS THE BEST PLAY

Say a good player (let's call him Mr. Pro) is playing no-limit Texas Hold 'em and he is heads-up with a very poor player (let's call him Mr. Amateur). Mr. Pro has a very good read on Mr. Amateur and he (Mr. Pro) knows that he is a 55 percent favorite in the hand (based on the hand Mr. Pro is holding and the hand he is quite certain that Mr. Amateur is holding). To Mr. Pro's surprise, Mr. Amateur puts all of his chips in the pot. Mr. Pro has enough money to cover the bet, but it would represent almost his entire bankroll. Mr. Pro's first reaction is to call, since he has the better hand. In fact, against a strong opponent,

Mr. Pro would not think twice about calling. So why shouldn't he call? Because there is still a 45 percent chance Mr. Pro could lose. Against a strong opponent, those odds are worth it. However, against a poor player, it is extremely likely that Mr. Pro will get plenty more chances to take Mr. Amateur's money when Mr. Pro is an even bigger favorite. So it does not make sense for Mr. Pro to risk his entire stake now. He should wait and save his bankroll for a better opportunity.

You cannot invest your time and money in every opportunity that comes your way. Be discriminating and take only the best ones that come your way. Think of your opportunity costs. Time and money invested in one opportunity is time and money that cannot be invested in the next opportunity.

AVOID PLAYING WITH MARGINAL HANDS

The money you do not lose at the poker table is as important as the money you win. The difference between winning and losing is often the amount of money you save by not playing losing hands. Good players avoid dangerous situations. They avoid marginal hands that can turn into playable but losing hands. Experienced players do not need action. They play to win, not just to play. They know to throw away trouble hands. Sure, they may throw away some potential winners, but overall they will save an awful lot of losers. Many beginning players cannot resist playing any ace in Texas Hold 'em. That is, they will play hands like ace-seven of different suits. Then when the flop brings an ace, they cannot fold the hand. The problem with this type of hand is that there is a high probability that another player will have an ace with a higher kicker. (A kicker is a side card that can count as part of your five-card hand. For instance, if you have ace-seven and your opponent has ace-nine and the flop comes ace-ten-two, you both have a pair of aces, but your opponent's nine is a better kicker than your seven.) When that happens, the inexperienced player will lose a lot of money. Good players avoid playing with marginal hands. They would rather wait and save their chips for a hand when they have an advantage. Weak players want action. They want to play rather than win. This is a losing proposition.

Avoid playing losing hands in your life. There are plenty of opportunities to choose from. If you have doubts about an investment, then you are most likely looking at a marginal hand. Sure, some of those investments you avoid may turn out to be winners, but overall your expected rate of return will be low. You will be much better served saving your chips for an investment you feel strongly about. Your goal should be to make money, not invest for the sake of investing.

If you receive a bonus from work, you do not have to invest it right away. Take your time and wait for a winning hand. Be smart and disciplined and follow your investment strategy. Avoid the pressure to get in the game at any cost. Make sure that when you play, the price is right. Remember that the money you do not lose is as important as the money that you win.

BALANCE GAIN VERSUS RISK

Unless you have the nuts in poker, every time you make a move you balance gain versus risk. Since poker is a game of imperfect information, players must take calculated risks. In addition to a solid fundamental understanding of poker math, the good player must use his experience, reads, and instinct to decide the probability of winning a pot and if the amount of money in the pot justifies that probability. For example, all things being equal, the top player knows to call a bet when he is a five-to-one underdog to win the pot if he will get paid six to one if he wins. Even though he is highly likely to lose that particular hand, he knows if he consistently makes that call, he will win money overall.

While this concept seems simple enough, decisions are not made in a vacuum. Many other factors need to be weighed when balancing gain versus risk. If you have a short stack of chips and you are up against a weak, loose player, you may not want to call that same bet as in the previous example. (A weak, loose player is someone who plays a lot of hands passively—they call bets frequently with inferior hands.) You are better off saving your money, since the weak, loose opponent is likely to give you plenty of opportunities to win money when you are a heavy favorite. If you are playing a tournament, the balance of risk versus gain is entirely different from that in a regular game. There are times in a tournament when chip preservation is more important than anything else, and there will be times when you must take a chance in order to survive. Once you are out of chips in a tournament, you are eliminated. In a regular cash game, you can always reach into your wallet and buy more chips if need be. That is why many otherwise good players have a hard time adjusting to tournament play.

When assessing whether to take a risk, you must consider the probability that you are right against the consequences if you are wrong. Avoid investments that provide limited upside with significant risk. For example, stay away from investing a lot of money in very big, troubled companies. Even if you think the company will turn around, if the company is already very big, your upside is probably limited. Though the investment may be worth some amount of money, it is not worth risking a lot to win a little. Conversely, small investments in tiny, risky companies may be worth the risk. Anyone making such an investment would have to be prepared to lose her entire investment, but the upside could be tremendous. Thus, a small investment could turn into a big return. Many savvy investors often find a handful of small, promising (albeit risky) companies to invest in. They realize that there is a very good chance that most, if not all, of the companies could go belly up. However, if only one of the companies does well, their overall return could still be tremendous.

Every individual must decide his or her own tolerance for risk. To help in that deliberation, make a careful consideration of the potential consequences before deciding if the risk is worth it.

There is a risk/gain analysis in most everything we do. Some things (i.e., an investment) are easier to quantify than others (i.e., whether to bring up a new topic in a business meeting when you are not sure how it will be perceived), but it doesn't mean the analysis is not present. Whether you are pursuing a new job or making a decision at your current one, take the time to go through a risk/gain analysis. The more you get accustomed to this exercise, the more natural it will become and the easier it will prove to quantify. Just be careful not to overanalyze any situation.

IT IS LESS COSTLY TO GIVE SOMEONE THE BENEFIT OF THE DOUBT THAN CASH

A healthy amount of skepticism is an admirable quality at the poker table. But too much cynicism, however, can be extremely expensive. The chronic cynic should steer clear of the poker room. She will never believe anyone. She will believe everyone is bluffing all of the time and this will cost her a lot of money. Rather than fold to a strong hand, she will bet or call. While poker is a game of imperfect information, the ability to assess situations in order to determine if an opponent is bluffing or not will come with experience. Such a decision should be based on objective reasoning—not cynicism. It is far better to give someone the benefit of the doubt than your hard-earned cash.

The stock market bust and related corporate scandals that followed the late nineties boom market has left many investors understandably skittish. To the extent that this has made investors more discriminating, this is a positive. However, investors need to avoid being overly cynical. Make investments based on extensive research and sound business judgment. Be critical but not totally untrusting. Every decision to invest involves some leap of faith. The extreme cynic would literally hide all of his cash under his mattress or bury it in his backyard. Of course, a depression-era investing mentality such as this would be disastrous. The costs in opportunity of being such a cynic would never allow you to put your money to work for you.

Be smart and disciplined in your investment choices. Be discriminating, but be careful that you do not become so cynical that you are afraid to invest in anything.

ADJUST YOUR PLAY—BUT DO NOT CONFORM

Experienced poker players know how to adjust their play. How they play against a weak, loose player is very different from how they would play against a tight, aggressive player. The good player is constantly adapting to the ever-changing circumstances at the poker table. He adjusts to take maximum advantage of the situation; he is careful not to conform to the pattern of the other players.

An example here might help illustrate this concept. Every poker table has its own natural rhythm. Typically, when a new table opens up, all of the players start out playing very tight: some of the players are trying to figure each other out and are proceeding cautiously. Others have promised themselves that they are going to play conservatively and avoid going on tilt (a player on tilt is playing worse than usual due to emotions clouding his judgment). After about a half hour or so of play, however, the table is usually a lot looser. All good intentions go out the window. Once there are a few contested pots, everyone seems to loosen up. Players feed off of the action of the table and loosen up in unison. The good player takes advantage of this. He will be overly aggressive early on to take advantage of his opponents' tentativeness. As his opponents loosen up, the good player will tighten up and wait to play strong hands, knowing that he will be paid off by the now loose players.

Professional investors know how to adjust to changing market conditions without conforming. If they sense a bull market beginning, they will get more aggressive. Bull markets tend to work the same as a new poker table. A bull market begins slowly and then progresses before anyone realizes it is under way. Investors, like players, loosen up as they witness more and more action. As the money flows faster and easier, even steady, well-reasoned investors may abandon their disciplined strategy. They are no longer content to stand on the sidelines. Finally, nearly everyone joins the frenzy, hoping to make easy money. A herd mentality overtakes the market as everyone jumps in. All bull markets end with everyone on tilt. The savvy few who can avoid conforming will make money. They will sell close to the top and buy close to the bottom by adjusting but not conforming.

ONE'S WILLINGNESS TO ACKNOWLEDGE A PAINTING IS A FAKE IS USUALLY INVERSE TO THE PRICE ONE PAID TO BUY IT

I do not know how many times I have seen the following situation at a no-limit poker table. Player A has about $20 invested in the pot when Player B makes a $100 bet on the river (after the last card is placed down). Player A calls with a hand he knew should have been a loser. When Player B turns over his winning hand, Player A defensively states something along the lines of "Well, I had to call since I was pot committed." Huh? A few hands later, that same Player A will call a $5 pot on the river. This time, when Player A loses, he says, "Boy, was that dumb. I knew you had it. I don't know why I called."

What happened between the first and second hands? Did Player A find true introspection during that time? Probably not. What is more likely is that Player A has a much easier time admitting a little mistake as opposed to a huge mistake. It is tough to analyze one's game in an honest fashion. No one likes to acknowledge mistakes, and the bigger the mistake, the harder the acknowledgment.

Have the courage to be honest with yourself when it comes to poker or evaluating your investments. Anyone can admit small mistakes. The ability to acknowledge large mistakes will give you the freedom to learn and progress. If you have made a risky investment in a stock that has gone south, admit the mistake, no matter how painful it may be. By doing this, you can sell and salvage something and move on. To not admit the mistake will only lead to a compounding of the mistake. You will not sell and may lose more. Worse yet, you may even buy more in the hopes of getting even. It is better to bruise your ego a little than your bank account a lot.

POKER IS A GAME OF INFINITE POSSIBILITIES

The possibilities in a game of poker are limitless. Every hand is unique. If you factor in the countless permutations in how the cards can be dealt, the pool of potential players, and the different ways players can react, then you can begin to understand how infinite the possibilities really are. Even if you somehow, against all odds, find yourself in a hand with the exact same players and the exact same cards are dealt to everyone and the betting limits are exactly the same both times, this will still be a unique experience. At least some of the players are sure to play the hand differently. Why? They may remember the previous hand and mix up their play. The hands before will be different, and this hand will present itself in a different context. Each player's chip stack will be different. Each player's understanding of the other players' play may have changed. Every player has had more experience in the interim. The players could be in a different mood. These are just a few of the factors that could make this hand play out differently.

If every hand is unique, how does one ever know for sure how to play a particular hand? The bottom line is: one rarely does. All you can do is rely on experience and your analysis of the current situation to make the best possible decision you can make. There is no substitute for experience. The more you play, the more you learn. The more you learn, the easier it will be for you to recognize a variety of situations and react to them. Even though every situation is unique, many will be similar, and experience will be your guide.

In investing, as in poker, there is no substitute for experience. Many people lost a lot of money in the stock market downturn that began in the year 2000. The similarities between the 1990s stock bubble market and the 1920s stock market bubble are numerous. Of course, very few people investing in the '90s had any firsthand knowledge of the '20s boom and bust. If more people had, things may have been different. Many investors in the '90s had never even experienced a bear market of any kind. For many, the only investing experience they had was one of great and rapid appreciation. Speculation and risk were greatly rewarded, while patience and discipline were left behind. We all know now, however, how the story ends. Speculation and risk crashed hard. While every bull and bear market is different, experienced investors are much better equipped to spot and analyze both opportunities and warning signs. They rely on their past experience to recognize current market conditions.

EVERYTHING REVERTS TO THE MEAN

Poker can be a very streaky game. There are times when it seems like you can do no wrong. You start with great hands that hold up. If you need a miracle card on the river, you catch it. Conversely, there are times when nothing seems to fall your way. Great starting hands never hold up. Your opponents always draw out on you. (That is, they stay in a hand with inferior hands and catch cards to beat you.) You never catch anything when you need it. Poker is a very idiosyncratic game, and the deviations from the mean can be tremendous. Experienced poker players realize, however, that everything is temporary. Hot streaks and cold streaks will come and go. Everything will eventually come to pass and revert back to the mean. Experienced players do not let hot or cold streaks affect their play. They do not gain false confidence when things are going their way and they do not get dejected or go on tilt when they suffer bad beats. This does not mean that they do not adjust their play accordingly. The experienced pro will use a good run of cards to intimidate his opponents. He will play them to maximum effect without getting carried away or thinking he is invincible.

Conversely, when things are going bad, the experienced pro may tighten up to minimize his losses. He does not try to win all of his money back at once. He does not get loose or sloppy. Throughout any streak, top players know to maintain their discipline and stay within their game, because they know that eventually everything reverts to the mean.

Maintain perspective when investing your hard-earned cash. Things are seldom as bad or as good as they seem. Do not get carried away chasing the latest trends. What's hot today will eventually come back to earth. The world is a random and idiosyncratic place. Oil prices can rise with the whims of a handful of people. Inflationary pressures can pop up and then dissipate. The dollar can rise and fall against other currencies. Natural disasters can temporarily affect anyone and anything to varying degrees. Stock prices can rise fast and furiously on nothing more than momentum. To constantly change your strategy with every passing event would be disastrous. Sure, you should keep up with key global lasting changes, however, you must distinguish real change with temporary blips.

Everything ebbs and flows before reverting to the mean. Maintain a rational and steady outlook. During the good times, however, take time for reflection. Recall some bad times so you can save and prepare for any bad times in the future. When things are going poorly, keep everything in perspective. Do not allow yourself to get paralyzed with fear. The worst decisions are those made out of fear. Recall some good times and remind yourself that this, too, shall pass. Everything, in business and in cards, eventually reverts to the mean.

Good sound business judgment works. Short-term fixes do not. Ignoring a problem or trying to fix it with a Band-Aid approach only prolongs the agony. Say you are having trouble with an employee who has repeatedly demonstrated a poor attitude and is negatively affecting the morale of his co-workers. Yet, crunch time for your company is coming up, and you know it will take some time to replace him. So, you decide that it's best to hold steady and hope this employee straightens out after yet another talking to. But you know that it is unlikely. You are only prolonging a problem and could be potentially causing more. Making the right decision is always right, even if there are some difficult short-term consequences.

PLAY THE SITUATION, NOT YOUR CARDS

Early on in my poker playing days, I learned a valuable lesson. I was playing seven-card stud, and there were four of us involved in a rather big pot. After the sixth card, the player to act first (let's call him Player A) appeared to hit his straight. Fortunately for me, I happened to catch a full house (which was not apparent, since two of my cards were face down). I was second to act. The two players behind me (Players C and D) both appeared to be drawing to flushes. A flush is better than a straight but not as good as a full house. Player A acted first and bet out. I immediately raised, since I had him beat. Players C and D both seemed surprised by my raise and folded. Since it was apparent that Player A had the straight and I was willing to raise, Players C and D correctly induced that I must have a very strong hand. Now, if I had just called, there is an excellent chance that Players C and D would have called as well, since the pot was large and if they hit their flush, they would be able to beat the straight. So by raising, I did get another bet out of Player A, but I lost two bets (one each from Players C and D). Additionally, I lost the opportunity to get more bets out of Players C and D after the seventh and final card. If either or both of Players C and D had made their flush on the seventh card, they may have been tempted to raise, and I could have made quite a few more bets. However, by forcing them to fold, I never gave myself that chance. I did not play the situation to maximum benefit. Rather, I played my cards and reacted without giving adequate thought to the entire situation.

In poker, your cards are only good in relation to the situation. A strong but losing hand should be folded. A weak hand can be played for profit if you sense your opponents are weak as well. The good player recognizes opportunities to exploit regardless of the cards that he is holding. When the good player does have the best hand, he sizes up the situation to make sure he maximizes his profit.

Do not play your cards blindly. Look at the big picture. When investing, research the competition to your potential investment. Look at industry trends and how your target company is adapting. Investment choices should always be made on future potential not past performance. No matter how strong a company may look, there may be a competitor emerging who is even stronger.

POKER IS A MARATHON, NOT A SPRINT

Even the best poker players in the world will have losing sessions. Such is the nature of the game. There will be days when the cards are just not falling right or that top player is not making correct reads on her opponent. To the experienced player, however, that is okay. They recognize that success in poker is measured over the long term. Players can be up or down in the short term due to a lot of factors other than skill. In the long run, however, skill will win out when those other factors even out. The experienced player does not get flustered by short-term defeats. Rather, she will stay the course and play her game, confident in her ability to eventually win out. On the other hand, the inexperienced player will look for the quick gain. He will play hands that he should not play. He will attempt to draw out in the hopes of winning a big pot even when he is a big underdog. This type of player is relying on luck, not skill, to win. There will, of course, be sessions when the cards fall right and this player wins. In the long run, however, he is guaranteed to lose.

If you are looking for financial success, think long term. Do not look for the quick fix. Do not get caught up with chasing the latest hot investment. Just like the weak poker player trying to draw out, the cards will fall your way occasionally, and you will win some money. In the long run, however, this is a losing proposition. You will end up playing too many hands when you face long odds. You would be much better off putting your money to work for you in areas where you have an edge. Rely on your skill to find a suitable investment that you completely understand. Do this consistently and in the long term, you will find success.

Investing, like poker, takes patience and discipline. You do not have to play the first hand you are dealt if you are not happy with the cards. Wait for the right opportunity when you sense you have a real advantage. You want to maintain diversity, but you still want to invest the most in your strongest hands.

THE POKER EXPERIENCE

In Over My Head

After my first introduction to poker, I was hooked, although it was extremely difficult to find anyone to play with on a consistent basis. It wasn't until high school that I would be able to play in a formal game with real money at stake, and it would not be until college that I could participate in a few regular games. During that time, however, I never played outside of private low-stakes games with friends.

After my first year of college, I was home for the summer. Our local parish church had a week-long carnival every summer and they offered seven-card stud poker in a smoky back room. I had been too young to participate in prior years, but this summer my brother-in-law Jim and I decided to give it a go. Being in a foreign environment was somewhat intimidating, especially since all of the other players were substantially older than me. This was the summer of 1982, well before the current poker craze, and just about anybody of my age had better things to do than play poker. Poker then was largely played by retirees and fringe society.

Being a college student working for minimum wage, I'm sure I had the smallest bankroll of anyone in the room. I think I had $25 in my pocket, which may not sound like much, however, at $1 to $2 a pop, *that could pay for a lot of keg parties. Or, equally important, it could buy used books for two classes for the upcoming semester. It was significant money to me.*

The game was seven-card stud. We would each post a twenty-five-cent ante, which the dealer would scoop off the table and keep for the church. For the first two rounds of each hand, betting would be fifty cents per bet with a maximum of three raises. For the last three rounds, the stakes would increase to $1 per bet. It didn't take me long to realize that the players were very loose. In seven-card stud, you are dealt three cards—two of them being down cards, meaning no one else could see them, and one card exposed—before any betting took place. Thus, for your twenty-five-cent ante, you got to see three out of the potential seven cards you could receive. With loose players betting freely, I decided early on to fold all but the most playable of hands. Even if you had a good starting hand, you had to be careful because if you didn't improve, you were likely to lose. Just about every hand had at least four players in it until the end. With this kind of style, there was a lot of luck involved. If you were going to win, you had to play somewhat cautiously, but you also had to be willing to gamble.

I ended up playing too scared, which culminated in a disastrous situation for me. I was slowly bleeding away my bankroll when I received a starting hand of two concealed threes with an ace up top. Since no one else had an exposed ace, I decided to play. The fourth card brought another three. I now had trip threes (three three's), which was a very strong hand. The fact that two of those threes were concealed greatly increased my opportunity to win a big pot, since other players would have a hard time figuring out what I had. Just as I hoped, there was betting and raising up to the maximum. A big pot was building. The next card did not improve my hand although I was still confident that I had the best hand. Again, there was more betting and raising to the maximum. Now a really big pot with well over $40 in it was before me.

The sixth card did not improve my hand, and I became nervous. I thought I might be beat. There were still four other players in the *hand; one had four to a flush and a couple of others had exposed pairs. With so much money in the pot, though, it was still well worth playing. Even if I didn't have the best hand, I could still make a full house with the last card. More worrisome to me, though, was the fact that I was down to my last $5. If this round of betting maxed out, it would cost me $4. That would give me $1 to play the last round, and I knew it would cost me more than that. When I played with friends, if you ran out of money you either borrowed or quit. If you were in the middle of a hand when you ran out, then you were on credit for whatever amount it would cost you. If you lost that hand, then you owed the winner whatever you were short.*

Now, I found myself in a real predicament. I was not sure what the etiquette was here, but I was fairly certain that you could not play for credit. I thought about asking my brother-in-law for a loan, but I really did not want to lose more than the $25 I had brought with me. I did not have a lot of time to think about it, and before I knew it, it was my turn to act. I panicked and folded my hand. Sure enough, the betting maxed out. The seventh card was dealt, and since I was in last position, my folding did not affect the cards received by the other players so I would have the opportunity to see if I did the correct thing in folding. I did not. My brother-in-law Jim ended up winning the hand with three deuces. My trip three's would have won. The pot was over $60, which was a lot of money to me at the time. I was sick to my stomach and I got up from the table. As bad as these players were (other than Jim), I had no business playing in this game with my feeble bankroll. Jim graciously offered to loan me some money. I declined, knowing that I would be playing even more scared with borrowed money than I would with my own.

I still took some comfort in the fact that I made the right decision at the time due to the fact that I did not have any money to finish the hand and I would have been forced to fold anyway once I ran out of money. That delusion was quickly shattered, however. The game was being played "table stakes," which, unbeknownst to me at the time, is quite common in casinos and public card rooms. In fact, it is the norm *not the exception. Table stakes means that you can play with only the money or chips you have on the table. You can't reach into your pocket in the middle of a hand and take out more money or buy more chips. If you happen to run out of money in the middle of a hand, then you are all-in (you have bet your entire stack) for that amount. Any additional money put in the pot by other players that you can't match goes into a side pot, which you are ineligible to win. So, in the hand highlighted here, I would have been all-in on the last card and there would have been four other players who would have put in another $3 each for a side pot of $12. I would have won the main pot, and Jim would have won the $12 side pot.*

I had no business putting myself in a situation where I lacked such a basic understanding of the rules of the game. I learned a valuable lesson, though. If I am going to commit money to something, I want to make sure I understand all of the parameters. It's like signing a contract without reading the small print.

3. AVOIDING TILT: THE PSYCHOLOGY OF POKER AND INVESTING

STRIKE THE RIGHT BALANCE BETWEEN GREED AND FEAR

There is an old saying on Wall Street that bulls and bears make money while pigs get slaughtered. The implication is clear. Invest conservatively, maintain a disciplined approach, and don't get carried away. Now, contrast that philosophy with Gordon Gekko's speech from the 1987 film *Wall Street*, in which he infamously proclaimed, "Greed is good." Set aside for a moment the fate that awaits Mr. Gekko at the film's end and try to decide if there is any truth to his statement. Can greed ever be a positive attribute when it comes to investing?

Before we answer that question, let's take a look at the importance of greed in poker. Poker requires a careful balance to be struck between greed and fear. If you get too greedy at the poker table, you may enjoy some great short-term success, but sooner or later you will lose all of your chips. When greed takes over, the focus is no longer on making correct decisions but on making money. You will become unjustifiably optimistic that the right cards are going to fall your way. Even if those cards don't come, you will be irrationally confident that you can bet enough to chase your opponents out. You will be impatient. All you will think about is the money you can potentially win, with no regard to the money you can lose. When those things happen, you are putting your money to work in situations that are unfavorable to you.

Now, let's take a look at fear. If fear consumes you at the poker table, you are also guaranteed to lose. You cannot win at poker without some degree of risk tolerance. There's simply no way to avoid it. You cannot win chips from your opponents without putting some of your own chips in danger. While poker is a game of skill and the players who consistently make correct decisions will win in the long run, luck plays an important role in the short term. Good players concentrate on making correct decisions and not on the results. They will continue to bet in favorable situations even if they are losing. Fearful players will play not to lose. They'll commit chips only to a hand that they believe is a sure thing. They play scared. They are unduly pessimistic. They believe that their opponents have stronger hands than they do. They lack the confidence to bet and raise when they should. They are more concerned about not losing any more chips than they are about making correct decisions and committing their chips when the situations favor them.

How do you find the proper balance between greed and fear at the poker table? To answer that, let's look at a hypothetical poker game between two extreme players—Mr. Greedy and Mr. Fear. Mr. Greedy will be overly aggressive and bet and raise every single pot. Mr. Fear will consistently fold until he has a super strong hand. So for the majority of hands where Mr. Fear does not possess very strong cards, Mr. Greedy will win the pot. Those pots will be small ones, since Mr. Fear will only be losing his blinds (a blind is a forced bet made by one or two players to start the first round of betting). Once Mr. Fear has a strong hand, however, he will call a bet and may even raise. If Mr. Greedy continues to play that hand aggressively, we are going to end up with a large pot that Mr. Fear will in all likelihood win. If each player plays completely to form, Mr. Greedy will win a great number of small pots and Mr. Fear will win an occasional really big pot. Overall, they may end up close to even.

Now, let's give to both Mr. Greedy and Mr. Fear a certain level of reasonableness and common sense. Let's increase their awareness so that they realize their tendencies. Both players will maintain their general disposition toward greed and fear, respectively. However, both players are willing to make small adjustments if they have the confidence to do so. In other words, we are not now talking about two totally stereotypical extreme players but real-life human beings with natural tendencies, albeit with the ability to reason. Which player do you think will do better?

Mr. Greedy is going to remain aggressive until he meets resistance. Mr. Fear will remain passive until he has strong cards or he gets tired of Mr. Greedy pushing him around. In this scenario, Mr. Greedy is going to continue to win a great number of small pots. However, when Mr. Fear now fights back, Mr. Greedy is more likely to let go of his hand, since he knows that Mr. Fear plays only strong hands. So when Mr. Fear wins his occasional pot now, it is likely to be a small one as well. With Mr. Greedy's winning a great number of small pots and Mr. Fear's winning only the occasional small pot, Mr. Greedy will ultimately prevail.

This is, of course, an oversimplification, but the point is still valid. Ask any poker player who they would back in the above scenario and you will get a consensus on Mr. Greedy. Greed will crush fear at the poker table every single time. When you sit down to the felt, a healthy—but not extreme—amount of greed is good. Many pots will be uncontested or up for grabs, so the player who goes after it will win it. When it comes to poker, anyway, Gordon Gekko was right. To find the proper balance between greed and fear, the starting point should be with greed. Fear is not a positive attribute at the poker table. Since we know that unbridled greed is a losing proposition, the goal then becomes one of tempering your greed to find the sweet spot of maximizing your return. How far you temper it will depend on the situation. Against a table of fearful opponents, you will be thriving on greed. Against top-notch competition, your greed should be tempered greatly although not quashed.

Now, let's get back to investing. If your primary goal is capital preservation, this conversation is not relevant. You should be investing in some very conservative fixed income accounts. However, if your goal is appreciation, then I believe the starting point has to be with greed. If you are more concerned with not losing money than you are with making money, then you are setting yourself up for failure. You're not going to make correct decisions in putting your money to work for you—especially at the most optimal times.

In poker, we need to temper our greed the most when we're up against the toughest competition and tap that greed when we're up against weak competition. This is a natural thing to do. It feels right once you're more experienced in the game. When investing, we must tap into greed when things appear bleakest and temper that greed when things often appear the rosiest. This is not a natural thing to do, and it is hard to overcome your opposite urges. The oldest and truest investing maxim in the world is still "buy low, sell high." When prices are low, the markets are getting hammered, consumer sentiment is down, and the outlook is bleak. Feelings of fear are going to dominate, and it is going to take a lot of willpower to find that greedy inner self so you can make some money.

When markets are booming and you're enjoying double-digit growth and the outlook has never appeared brighter, it's easy to let greed take over. If not controlled, that greed can become unbridled and lead to disaster. That is the time to temper your greed and try to divorce your emotional state from your decision-making process. Look at economic realities and make correct decisions based on fundamental investment principles. Your concentration during these times should be on making correct decisions, not on making money.

Just as emotions can overwhelm your decision-making process, they can also influence the market at large. Markets tend to get overbought and oversold based on investor sentiment. When decisions are being unduly influenced by others' emotions, an opportunity exists. Exploit that opportunity. At the poker table, the time to be aggressive is when everyone else is playing scared. In the stock market, the time to be aggressive is when everyone else is timid.

Don't be afraid to voice your opinion at work even if it is counter to the prevailing popular opinion. Following the herd is easy. Bucking the trend is courageous. Of course, don't say the opposite for opposite's sake. However, if you feel strongly about something, speak up.

WAIT FOR A BETTER HAND

You do not have to play every hand you are dealt. If you do not believe that the situation is advantageous for you, fold your cards. A new hand will be dealt in just a few short moments. You will have the opportunity to start anew. A new opportunity will be there for you to evaluate. Though the next one may not prove advantageous, that is okay. Fold that one, too. If you crave action, go play slots with the realization that the house has a huge edge. If you want to play winning poker, however, then be patient. Wait for a hand when you perceive an advantage. It will come. You may not win that hand, but if you consistently play those hands in which you perceive an advantage and discard the others, you will soon find your bankroll increasing.

There are probably plenty of areas in your life where you are already practicing the concept of waiting for a better hand. When new electronics and gizmos come out, we all realize that the prices will come down drastically over time. Thus, the majority of us wait for the price reductions before purchasing. We have come to expect great savings in post-holiday sales that we wait for and take advantage of.

We tend to forget the concept, however, when emotions are running high. If we are looking for a new home, we are tempted to bid on the first home we see and love. When a favorite stock is taking off, we are worried that we are going to miss out on all of the gains. We are incredibly fortunate to live in a time of ever-expanding opportunities. The twenty-first century is proving to be one with a true global market and instant access to information through technological developments. It has never been easier to wait for a better hand. New opportunities can be researched and found in a matter of moments.

DO NOT PLAY IN A HIGHER STAKES GAME THAN YOU CAN AFFORD

A cardinal rule of poker that applies equally to recreational players and professionals is that one should never play in a higher stakes game than one can afford. Always play within your means. The first reason for this is simple and obvious enough. No one should blow money on a card game that is needed for other purposes. Only disposable income set aside for entertainment purposes should be bet. The other reason is not so obvious, but it is just as important. When you play in a higher stakes game than you can afford, your judgment is often impaired. Since you cannot afford to lose, you will likely play differently. You will lack confidence. You will be playing not to lose instead of to win. Whenever you play not to lose, you are guaranteed to lose. Poker players can smell scared money a mile away and they will pounce all over it.

That's why it is so critical for poker players to play a game that they can easily afford. In such a game, players play with confidence and they are not afraid to put their chips to work. They will not be easily scared out of a pot. They will make smart decisions when they are not feeling a ton of pressure playing with money they cannot afford to lose.

A good rule of thumb in investing is to always stay within your means. Do not buy a house that will stretch your monthly income beyond its limits. When people try to do things outside of their means, their judgment will be impaired. Instead of getting a fixed-rate mortgage, they will go for a one-year adjustable that leaves them very vulnerable to any rise in interest rates.

Do not make investments that you cannot afford to hold onto for a few years at least. If you invest not to lose, you greatly increase the risk that you will lose. You are more likely to panic and sell at the bottom when you cannot afford to wait it out. You are playing with scared money, which is never a good thing.

Always allocate your finances and assets in a manner that is well within your means. This will afford you the time for thoughtful, reasoned analysis and allow you to make smart decisions. When your financial well-being is not in jeopardy, you will not feel pressured into making bad choices.

PLAYING POKER IS NOT DANGEROUS; PLAYING POKER POORLY IS DANGEROUS

You are not going to win every time you play poker. There will be plenty of times that you lose. Even the best players lose. That does not mean that playing poker is dangerous or even a losing proposition. Nothing worthwhile in life is without risk. Good poker players are able to withstand the risk and the short-term swings to become profitable overall. Poor players will never be profitable in the long run. They may enjoy some short-term success, but for them, poker is a losing proposition. Unless the poor player can dramatically improve his game, he should give it up. For the poor player, poker is dangerous.

There is no such thing as a risk-free investment. Even fixed-rate funds or certificates of deposits have risk. While these investments certainly have minimal risk, the risk is your opportunity costs. If you invest 100 percent of your assets in a certificate of deposit yielding 3.75 percent per year, you run the risk that your interest will not even keep up with inflation. By refusing to invest in other potentially higher yielding investments, you have opportunity costs.

Everyone has to decide what is their own level of risk tolerance. Just as some people have no appetite for poker, there are plenty of people who have no desire to invest in individual stocks or more aggressive mutual funds. That does not mean that such investing is dangerous. If an investor is able to withstand the risk and the short-term swings to earn an above-market rate of return, I would say that investor is successful. However, if an investor consistently picks stocks that underperform, then he should either radically change his play or give it up. For that player, investing in stocks is dangerous.

Many poker players find success at certain levels of play. However, when they move up to higher betting limits where the risk is greater, they find that they cannot win. These players would be smart to stick to a level of play that allows them to be profitable. Investors should take note. Find investments that are within your comfort level for both skill and risk that will allow you to be profitable.

AVOID GOING ON TILT

To go on tilt in poker is to play recklessly. It is different from general poor play. A weak player will play badly because he does not know better. To go on tilt is to deviate from otherwise solid play. Even the best of players will occasionally go on tilt. Many things can cause this. Boredom, frustration, and bad beats are among the factors that can put a player on tilt. A bad beat is a hand you lose to an opponent who catches a miracle card to beat you when you are an overwhelming favorite.

A player can sit at the poker table for a long time without seeing many good hands to play. At that point, it takes willpower and discipline to avoid lowering his standards. The good players realize that the good hands will come if they are patient. Similarly, the business world has natural cycles. There are bull and bear markets. When you are in a bear market, do not lower your investment requirements. Be patient. Wait for the good hands to come. The money you do not lose is as important as the money you win. Do not get frustrated or bored with a bear market.

Strangely enough, success can also put a player on tilt. A good player gets a few decent hands in a row and his confidence grows. He gets involved in a couple of hands that he should have folded, yet he wins those hands by getting lucky. The nature of poker is that poor play will sometimes be rewarded. Instead of counting his blessings and straightening out his play, the player may now think he is invincible. He now believes that he will draw out a winning hand every time. He is on tilt. He is sure to lose everything he just won and more if he does not get back to steady, disciplined play.

The excessive bull market of the late '90s put even the savviest of investors on tilt. Investors could do no wrong. Even picking stocks with no earnings and inexperienced management would pay off. Investors' mistakes were rewarded by an overwhelming bull market. Those investors who failed to get back to steady, disciplined investing lost all of their gains and then some.

The most common factor that puts a player on tilt is a bad beat. A bad beat happens when you have a strong hand beaten by an opponent who was a big underdog but made a lucky draw. This is especially true when your opponent is playing poorly and should not have been in the pot in the first place. How players react to a bad beat will go a long way in determining their ultimate success. Bad beats are a fact of life in poker. The experienced player who recognizes this will stay emotionally detached and not steer course from his normal disciplined play. Still, poker players are human. Despite the best of intentions, just about every player will get upset at the poker table at one time or another. When a player lets his emotions get the best of him, he is in serious trouble. He plays way too many hands in the hopes of making his money back. He starts throwing chips around indiscriminately at the poker table. He is on tilt.

Take control of your finances in real life. We all make mistakes. If your debt is starting to pile up, do not get frustrated and throw in the towel. Do not throw good money after bad. If you make an unsound investment, do not try to make it up all at once by chasing another bad investment. Instead, regroup and go back to a sound, disciplined investment strategy. If you have credit card debt, consider a home equity loan to consolidate your debt at a lower rate than your credit cards. In that case, look for the lowest fixed-interest rate available and consult with an accountant to see if your interest payments are deductible.

DO NOT LET YOUR EMOTIONS GET THE BEST OF YOU

In all areas of finance or poker, don't let your emotions take over. Poker is a cold, calculating game. The best players are those who can remain emotionally detached and play with discipline and control. They treat each hand individually. They avoid playing marginal hands even if they have not received anything playable in quite some time. They do not get overconfident when they are on a winning streak. The good player recognizes that there will be times when he can exploit his opponent's vulnerabilities even when the good player does not have a good hand. There will be other times when the good player will lay down a flush when he knows he is up against a bigger flush. The good player does not feel pressured to win his money back when he is down. Rather, he remains objective and continues to play smart, knowing that his strategy is effective over the long haul. The good player gets a read on his opponents but he does not let his opponents get under his skin.

It is extremely hard to remain emotionally detached at the poker table. You are competing in a game that involves both skill and luck and you are judged by how much money you are up or down. It is easy to get discouraged when you are down. Even if you have suffered some bad luck, your ego will be bruised. It is just as easy to gain a false sense of confidence when things are going your way. You look at that big stack of chips in front of you and you can easily think that you are invincible. Whenever you get emotional in poker, you make mistakes. You play hunches instead of your opponents. You attack an opponent because you are ticked off, not because you feel you have an edge. You chase runners believing that you are due for a winning hand. You call an opponent who you know has a stronger hand because you are sick of seeing him win. In short, you make emotional decisions instead of objective decisions based on your read of the situation.

In a similar way, remain emotionally detached in your investment decisions. It is easy to get discouraged if you bought a stock right before a market correction. Conversely, if you have a few runaway winning stock picks, it is easy to forget that stocks can go down as easily as they can go up. Do not invest on hunches. Do not try to win all of your money back if you are down. Do not try to keep up with how much money your neighbor tells you he is making. Adopt an investment strategy that works for you and stick with it. Be objective, do your research, and make decisions based on individual company prospects and overall market conditions.

In today's work environment, it sometimes feels as though every waking moment we're either working or reachable via cell phone or e-mail. We all lose patience at times and find our nerves frayed. If you are working long hours on a project, it's very easy to personalize it. To a large extent, that's a good thing. Taking ownership and responsibility will propel you to do your very best. There is a very fine line there to keep in mind. When something gets so personalized, it's hard to retain objectivity and emotional detachment. Remember that criticism is constructive and meant to improve performance. Reasonable people can have differing opinions. If you detach yourself from taking criticisms personally, it will be much easier to keep your composure and remain a valued employee.

Learn to Deal with Luck

The uninformed may argue otherwise, but poker is a game of skill. As anyone who has played can attest, however, there is a fair amount of luck involved. There will be hands where you do everything right but lose due to your opponent's lucky draw. In the short term, you can experience both good and bad streaks. There will be times when the cards are running well and there will be times when the cards are running bad. How a player handles the bad luck will go a long way to determining his ultimate success. Most players know how to play good cards. What separates the winning player from the losing one is her ability to handle bad cards. How she plays bad cards and how she reacts to bad luck will be indicative of her likely success over the long term. The good player remains emotionally detached. She does not allow bad luck to affect her overall play. She remains committed to her solid, disciplined strategy.

Luck plays a significant part in investing. How we handle it goes a long way to determining our ultimate success. You can do everything right and still lose sometimes. For example, say you invest in the stock of a blue chip semiconductor company after doing as much due diligence as you could. Soon after your investment, news hits that one of the company's manufacturing facilities in Taiwan has been decimated by an earthquake. As a result, the company's manufacturing capacity will be materially impaired for at least nine months, and the stock sells off 30 percent on the news. What do you do? First of all, you do not go on tilt. You do not sell in a knee-jerk reaction. You do not buy more thinking it cannot go down any further. You reevaluate the company's prospects based on the latest developments and stock price. Wait at least a few days for the news to get absorbed by the market and then make an informed decision when the market for the stock is once again based on reason.

You never know when bad luck will hit. While you cannot control bad luck, you can prepare for it. Diversify your investments for this very reason. A well-diversified portfolio lessens the impact of such bad news. Investing, like poker, is situational. Depending on such factors as your age, number of dependents, amount of savings, and tolerance for risk, how you diversify will vary. A good financial consultant can certainly help you, but remember, as some of those factors change, you will need to make adjustments.

THE GAMBLER'S FALLACY

A common mistake gamblers make is to believe that they are due. That is, if a coin is flipped ten times and it comes up heads ten times in a row, many people falsely believe that the probability of the next flip being tails is much greater than it being heads. Of course, the odds are

50/50 the next flip will be either heads or tails. Each coin flip is completely independent of every flip that came before it. As easy as this concept is to understand, many either consciously or subconsciously ignore it. When playing poker, it is easy to believe that you are due for cards if you have not received anything playable for a while. Conversely, if an opponent has been getting good cards, you want to believe that their luck has to change. The problem with this way of thinking is that every hand is dealt independently of each other. Thus, you are under the delusion of the gambler's fallacy. How do experienced poker players manage to avoid falling prey to this fallacy? Quite simply, they do not gamble. While there is a great amount of luck in poker, it is ultimately a game of skill. The good player knows that there can be short-term fluctuations in her bankroll due to the capriciousness of the cards. If she is down, she avoids going on tilt. She knows she does not have to win all of her losses back right away. Rather, as long as she continues to play smart and disciplined, she will be a winner in the long run. So instead of feeling she is due, the good player examines her play to make sure she is playing well and then stays the course. The poker player who relies on luck rather than skill is likely to bet bigger when he is down, under the mistaken belief that he is due and will get his money back.

Avoid a gambler's mentality when investing. If you invest in the stock of a company and it goes down, avoid the gambler's fallacy. Do not believe that the stock is "due" to rise. Many make this mistake and invest a lot more money in the stock in the hopes of making their money back. Typically when a stock price drops, it is symptomatic of a larger fundamental problem. Rather than throw more money at it, take the time to examine the company's financial condition and prospects. Reevaluate the investment and continue to make smart and disciplined decisions. Just because a stock has gone down ten days in a row does not mean that it is likely to rise on day eleven.

PLAY FROM THE GUT ONCE IN A WHILE

If the idea of playing from the gut once in a while seems at odds with not forcing the action, it is because to a certain extent it is. (Forcing the action is being aggressive when you do not perceive any advantage.) Poker, like life, is full of apparent paradoxes. That is because very few rules have universal application. Poker is an extremely complex game with infinite possibilities. While as a general rule one should not force the action when one does not have adequate information, one may not always have the luxury of waiting for adequate information before making a move. If you are playing poker with experienced players, they will be mixing up their play quite effectively, thereby limiting the times when you can put them on a hand. If you played only when you thought you had them figured out, you would be playing very few hands and you would be allowing your opponents to win too many hands without a fight. You must find a careful balance between not forcing the action and playing from the gut.

You cannot look at every house on the market in your price range. You cannot personally visit the corporate offices and interview all of the executive officers of that company whose stock you are interested in. You can only do what you can do and only you can decide what is enough information for you. At some point, the extra information to be gained is not worth the effort necessary to gain it. You must balance not forcing the action with making an instinctual decision. Sometimes, if something feels right in your gut, you must go with it. Your gut instincts are based on a lifetime of experience, so they are not always the thoughtless impulses that some fear them to be.

No matter what job you have, you have it because someone has confidence in you and believes that you are qualified. You must believe that you are qualified as well and plan for success, not failure. Trust your instincts and don't waver. If you have people who work for you, allow them to make decisions suitable for their position. Empower them to believe in themselves and trust their gut as well—

unless they consistently prove unreliable. Inaction is the worst possible decision.

THE POKER EXPERIENCE

A Matter of Guts

Upon graduation from law school, the father of my law school roommate offered him a free trip to Hawaii for two. Airfare from Chicago and hotel accommodations in Hawaii were included. My friend and roommate graciously invited me to join him for a much-needed week of relaxation before the serious study we'd be undertaking for the upcoming bar exam. (I'd be taking the New York state bar exam, which covered over thirty topics and would require the better part of two months of preparation.) Since I was staying at my parents' house in Wilmington, Delaware, for the summer, I had to pay for round trip airfare to Chicago. Since I had never been to Chicago, I went out a few days prior to our departure for Hawaii so we could go to a Cubs game and check out some of the sights, sounds, and nightlife of Chicago.

After a couple of days of that and facing a very early flight the next morning, we decided we should do something a little more low key our last night before takeoff. Now, my friend lived in a fairly wealthy suburb of Chicago. He invited some of his friends over for a game of poker. A fairly big group came over, and we ended up with a total of eight players. Now, all of these guys came from this same wealthy town and in addition had been working the last couple of years while I had been piling up debt attending law school.

The game was fast and loose with most of the players more intent on gambling and having a good time than concentrating on the skill required for poker. Even though we had our hotel and airfare accounted for, we would still need a couple of hundred dollars for local transportation, food, and nightlife. The cash I had with me was budgeted for the trip. Thus, I had to be fairly conservative in playing with my bankroll. If I lost, it wasn't going to be a fun trip.

The game was played for mostly modest stakes, and I was up maybe $30 as the night was coming to an end. We were playing dealer's choice, which meant that we took turns dealing with the deal rotating clockwise. When it was your turn to deal, you could deal any game you wanted. This was a common practice in home games long before no-limit Hold 'em tournaments became the norm. It provided a lot of variation even if I didn't always like the game chosen. For instance, some players always chose a game with a lot of wild cards, which greatly increased the luck factor. Others would even choose nonpoker games such as blackjack or acey-deucey. I really disliked these and would try to at least limit the offerings to poker. The players who usually dealt these games tended to be the weakest players, though. In any poker game, you have to give up some of your edge if you want to keep everyone else involved and playing, so I didn't argue too much.

Whenever I dealt, I chose one of two types of games. I would either choose a positional game that provided the dealer with a big edge or a game that focused on a strategy most others would not be that familiar with. So, all things considered, dealer's choice still offered the astute player an overall advantage. I would learn firsthand that night of some unanticipated perils.

The only constant of this home game, and most home games, is that no matter what game is being dealt, the stakes stayed the same or as close to the same as possible. If $1 was established as the maximum bet, then when it was your turn to deal, you couldn't suddenly change the stakes to a higher amount. Some games did have more betting rounds than others, but you could factor that in when determining how long to stay in a hand. There were, however, a few games that lasted longer than one hand. For instance, there is a popular five-card draw game called "jacks or better, trips to win." In this game, you cannot open the betting unless you have at least a pair of jacks, and you cannot win the pot unless you show at least three of a kind or you manage to bet everyone else out of the hand. Since it is unlikely that someone will win on the first hand, the same dealer will keep dealing until someone makes three of a kind. Because everyone is still putting in antes and bets every hand, the pot can get quite large. There is a huge incentive then to stay in every hand even if you don't have anything, because once you fold, you're out of that hand and all future hands until someone wins the pot. Even so, you always have the option of folding at any time and you can manage how much you are willing to risk.

There was one game played, however, where managing your losses became much more difficult even though the stakes remained the same. This game was called "Guts." There are many different variations of Guts. I had always played a two-card drop version. In this game, each player was dealt two cards face down. That is all the cards anyone gets. It is two-card poker, so a pair of aces is the best possible hand and any pair is still a good hand. Depending on how many players you have, ace high or even king high is a fairly good hand. The betting and, more important, how you win a pot in this game are dissimilar to any other poker game that I know. Everyone puts in an ante. Then the cards are dealt. Everyone looks at their cards and then holds them out in front of them about six inches above the table. The dealer will then instruct out loud, "One, two, three, drop." If you want to fold your hand, you drop your cards. If you want to play your hand, you hold onto them. All the players who hold onto their cards then turn them face up. The winner takes the money out of the pot. The loser(s) then match the pot for the next hand. If everyone drops, everyone antes again and you re-deal. The game doesn't end until only one person holds onto his cards. Even then, that person has to beat the top two cards from the deck. If he does, then he scoops the pot, and since there is no one else to match the pot, there is nothing left to play for. The pots, as well as the risk, can grow rather quickly in this game.

For example, say we have six players in the game and the antes are $1. You know that it will cost you exactly $6 if you stay and lose. Let's assume three players stay for the first hand. The winning player *takes the $6 out of the pot. The two losing players each put $6 in the pot for a total of $12. Before the next hand is dealt, each player again antes $1. Thus, there is now $18 in the pot, so if you stay and lose, it's going to cost you $18. The price of poker just got more expensive. A couple of more rounds of this, and the game can become very expensive. Of course, as it becomes more expensive, players are less likely to stay with anything less than a very strong hand. I liked this game because if the pot became quite large and I sensed the others were playing scared, I would stay with a less than strong hand in order to win a very large pot. It was a great game in judging risk versus reward and greed versus fear. More important, you really had to judge your opponents' risk tolerance. The less risk tolerance they had, the greater I would have. I never liked the "beating the deck rule," as it neutralizes your guts. If you know your opponents are playing scared, you still can't stay unless you have a hand that has a fairly good chance of beating the deck's random cards. At least in this version, regardless of how expensive the game becomes, each player could decide for himself how much risk he wants to take. If the amount of the pot becomes too large, you can simply fold everything but a pair of aces.*

That night in the suburbs of Chicago, I was introduced to quite a different version of Guts that greatly diminished a player's ability to manage his risk exposure. In this version, each player was dealt two cards face down and a third card face up. This was three-card poker, and the best hands in order were a straight flush, three of a kind, a straight, a flush, a pair, and then high card. Straights and flushes were of the three-card variety, and you will note that a straight beat a flush in this game, which is contrary to regular poker. The betting and how you win a pot was exactly the same as the two-card version. The big difference, however, was that there was not a drop in this game. Instead, the player with the lowest-ranking exposed card had to stay in the hand. Then, starting clockwise from that player, each player declared whether he was in or out. The player seated to the immediate right of the player with the exposed low card was in the best position. He could see how many players declared in before it was his turn to act. This game really required less guts than the two-card version because you had more available information before you acted. In the two-card version, everyone was essentially acting in first position, since they had no idea of who would stay or drop before they had to make a decision.

The worst thing about this game, though, was that you could lose a lot of money through no action or decision of your own. If you were dealt the low card up, you had no choice but to stay in. Not only did you have to stay in, you had to stay in with the worst starting card of everyone at the table. When the rules were explained to me, I immediately did not like the game, but I didn't protest too loudly. I was the outsider in this game and I was up a few dollars, so I didn't want to appear to be a bad sport. Sure enough, the pot increased quite dramatically in a short period of time. The way this game was set up, I honestly wasn't sure when, how, or if it would end. Theoretically, everyone could go broke before there was a winner. With two-card drop Guts, you are more likely to end up with a situation where only one player remains, since everyone makes a decision simultaneously. In this version, one person was staying no matter what, and the players in late position had the added benefit of knowing what everyone else did before acting. With eight players and $1 antes, we had a pot of close to $200 in what seemed like a very short amount of time. The very next hand, I had a three as my exposed card, which proved to be the low. I didn't even bother to look at my other cards since I had no choice to make and I didn't want to give off any tells. I'm sure I already looked panicked enough. If I lost this hand, my bankroll would not only be wiped out for the night but for the upcoming trip. I felt completely helpless and I hated it.

My despair gradually lessened as I watched player after player fold in turn. I couldn't believe it. There were only two more players left to act. The second-to-last player took his time, slowly torturing me with his deliberation. He finally stayed. The last player folded. At least I only had one hand to beat. He turned over an ace high. I still had a chance. I turned my cards over one at a time. My initial three was already up. I turned over the second card, which was an eight. No help whatsoever. With only one more card to turn over, I had to see a three or an eight. Anything else and my trip to Hawaii wasn't going to be much fun. The final card was another eight, and instead of celebrating, I immediately asked the table that we split the pot equally and end this game. Fortunately, I don't think my roommate wanted to risk his traveling bankroll any more than I did, and he quickly agreed. (Or, perhaps, he didn't want to see me lose my bankroll and ruin the upcoming trip by not being able to afford anything.) Anyway, since he was the host, no one objected. I took out the pot, the loser matched it, and then we divvied it up eight ways and called it a night. I never played that bastardized version of Guts again. I don't want anything to do with a game where I can lose a lot of money based on no action or inaction on my part. It's not poker, even if it did provide me with some extra cash in Hawaii.

4. TABLE LEADER: NEGOTIATE FROM POWER

W hen entering a poker tournament, I like to get to the casino early. I register early and avoid the long lines. Then I can get something to eat, relax, and review the blind structure. In every poker tournament, the players will start with a predetermined number of chips (that have no value outside of the tournament) and there will be a set blind structure that will increase at regular intervals. (For instance, the blinds may start at $25 to $50 and increase every thirty minutes.) These factors vary with every tournament but are critical in determining how you should play.

The way tournaments work is that increasing the amount of the blinds (and introducing antes that each player must post every hand) forces the action. Players cannot afford to sit back and wait for premium cards, or their stack will erode. Starting chip stacks in relation to the blinds will go a long way in determining how aggressive one needs to play at the outset. For instance, if you start with $10,000 in chips with the blinds at $25 to $50 and each level lasts one hour (before the blinds increase), then you have plenty of time to play poker. By the way, that is a typical structure for a major tournament that might take five days to play. In this kind of tournament, a player could start out slowly and get a feel for the game and her opponents.

By being very conservative early, she can take advantage of her tight reputation by turning on the aggression in the later, more expensive rounds. She's willing to concede some small pots early on in order to win much larger pots later.

Conversely, if the starting stacks are only $1,000 and the blinds still start at $25 to $50 but increase every fifteen minutes, then your approach should be entirely different. This would be a typical structure for a daily small buy-in tournament that might be over in six hours; you're going to have to be aggressive fairly early on or your stack will diminish quickly. Players don't have much choice but to fight for pots at the outset. By doing your homework ahead of time and being intimately aware of the structure throughout the tournament, you will be prepared to do what is necessary in order to stay ahead of the game.

Negotiation begins well before you engage the other side. Before you ever sit down, you should do your research. Know what the major discussion points will be and what arguments and counterarguments are likely to be articulated. Try to anticipate what issues will be most important to your adversary and how that matches up with your interests.

Just like in a poker tournament, every negotiation will have a structure. Unlike a poker tournament, you have the power to formulate that structure. For instance, you can steer the negotiations by addressing a couple of smaller issues up front that you are ready to concede. This allows you to feel out your counterpart and build up some goodwill. You can then capitalize on that goodwill by taking a hard stance on the issues most important to you.

Some negotiations may only have a couple of primary issues to discuss. This is going to be a fast-structure negotiation. You are going to have to be aggressive from the outset in stating your case. If you start out too tentative, your negotiating power will quickly erode, much like that short chip stack in our hypothetical tournament that had a quick structure.

In a poker tournament, you are assigned a table and a seat completely at random. I like to get to my table a good fifteen to twenty minutes before the tournament starts. Usually a couple of other players will be there as well, and I can engage them in some small talk. This allows me to study their mannerisms and visual cues while they have their guard down. I can ascertain how they act when they are comfortable and relaxed and talking with confidence. I may even steer the conversation to try to hit a hot button by bringing up a controversial political issue to see how this person reacts in a more uncomfortable environment. The visual cues I pick up are often consistent with tells (a mannerism that may indicate what a player is thinking) that they will unconsciously display during the poker tournament.

Ascertaining some tells is well worth the time spent. What's more amazing, though, is how often players voluntarily tell me how they play. Poker players are famous for sharing strategy and discussing hands. If you want to keep learning, it's a good practice to have a couple of close confidantes to discuss "all things poker." It's not a good idea, though, to volunteer information to a complete stranger who is going to be sitting across the felt from you in five minutes. Yet I can't believe how many times a player will make a comment like "I play straightforward poker" or "I'm going to either build up a big stack early or go bust." Sure, some of the times players are deliberately giving me false information (although that in and of itself is telling), but the majority of the times a player makes a comment like that, he's speaking the truth. This small talk isn't limited to the time period before the tournament starts. On breaks, I often ask players about specific hands played and get an honest response.

You can take the same approach in negotiating in a business situation. Before you get down to the nitty-gritty back-and-forth, have a cup of coffee, and make small talk. Look for visual cues and work in some probing questions about the matter at hand that may elicit a response. I can't guarantee that this tactic will always work, but I think you will be surprised at how often it does. This is especially true if there are multiple parties involved. People are more reluctant to share information about others than themselves.

In certain situations, you will have multiple businesspeople and a few attorneys on each side of the negotiating table. Not everyone is going to be on the same page. I try to elicit some information during breaks. Some people are all too willing to let it be known that they are not the ones holding up the progress. They will strongly intimate that a client is being unreasonable, in their opinion. Or, a businessperson may confess that she doesn't care about a point but her attorney is making a big deal out of it. Once you have that information, it's only a matter of time before the other side concedes the point.

Gathering as much information as possible in business is as critical as it is in poker. It's easy to understand your concern when certain information is hidden from you and some co-workers are doing everything in their power to not only hide that information from you but actively deceive you as to what that information is. Try to reach out to your colleagues. Let them know implicitly that you will share in the glory with them if you all succeed together. Co-workers can be an invaluable source of information. Everyone in a company has areas of knowledge and expertise. Tap into that knowledge for the overall good of the company. Get together informally with colleagues before an important meeting so that there are no surprises. Use downtime such as your lunch hour to pick the brains of others. Information is always critical and when it's readily available, it's foolish not to get it. There is a tendency to underestimate the value of information when it's readily available. Don't fall into that trap.

IF YOU ARE GOING TO CALL, THEN GO AHEAD AND BET

If there is an advantage to being the first one to bet, then it should follow that if you are willing to call a bet, you should go ahead and bet. If you are going to stay in the hand, you are much better off playing from strength rather than weakness. If you play from strength rather than from weakness, then you impose your will on your opponent and you have the advantage. For example, say you are playing Hold 'em. You are in the big blind holding the seven of clubs and the eight of hearts and you have one caller before the flop. The flop comes five of diamonds, eight of diamonds, nine of spades. Unbeknownst to you, your opponent has the queen of spades and the jack of spades, giving him an inside straight draw and two over cards. If you bet out first, your opponent will put you on a better hand and he may or may not call depending on the circumstances, since he does have a number of outs (cards that could come and improve his hand to a winning one). If the turn brings him no help and you continue to bet, it becomes more difficult for him to call. Finally, if the river brings no help and you continue to bet out, he has no choice but to fold (or try a risky bluff raise). By betting out, you have kept him on the defensive and he must decide each time whether to fold or pay for the opportunity that a future card will help him.

Now, suppose that after the flop instead of betting, you decided that with a middle pair and an inside straight draw you had a playable hand, but perhaps not the strongest, so you check. Your opponent immediately bets, and now you are on the defensive. You have to be the one to decide if it's worth calling or if your opponent has a better hand. Even if in both hypotheticals the amount of money bet is identical, you are in a vastly superior position in the first scenario where you bet out first. You stand a much greater chance of winning the pot if your opponent does not draw out. In the second scenario, you will face some very difficult decisions if you do not improve. If a scare card such as an ace or a third diamond fell on the turn, you would probably have to fold in the face of a bet from your opponent even though it did not help him. (These cards are considered scare cards because they could give your opponent a pair of aces or a flush.)

The biggest difference in the two scenarios is that in the first one you are using your chips as force. You are being the aggressor and putting your opponent on the defensive. In the second scenario, you are using your chips as currency to buy another card. Even though the amount you are wagering is exactly the same in both scenarios, you stand a much greater chance of winning when you play with strength and use your chips as force.

Be the one to take the lead in negotiations. Whenever you take the lead, you establish a position of strength, which can only help you control the negotiations. Taking the lead does not necessarily mean committing yourself to a position. For example, say you are at a garage sale and you see the exact baby jogging stroller you have been shopping for. The one you are looking at is in good condition, and you know that an identical stroller, also in good condition, sold recently for $75 on eBay. While you would be happy to pay the $50 asking price, you are sure you can get it for less. You can take the lead in one of two ways, depending on the situation. First, if your goal is to establish a price range well below the asking price and you have witnessed the seller to be a pretty firm negotiator, then ask the seller if he will accept $25. On the other hand, if you believe the seller is having a fire sale, ask him what he will take and see how far he will go down. Then work off that price. In both of these scenarios, you are taking the lead. Even though your tactic is different in each situation, in both of them you are acting first, which controls the negotiations.

IF YOU KNOW YOUR OPPONENT AND YOU KNOW YOURSELF, SUCCESS WILL FOLLOW

In poker it is equally important to know both yourself and your opponent. To be able to play successfully requires a thorough understanding of the game and to know one's own strengths and weaknesses. That is only half of the equation, however. If you are only able to play your own hand without any regard to how your opponent is playing, you cannot prevail over the long term. In order to defeat your opponent, you must be able to "put him on a hand." That is, you must study and analyze your opponent's playing style and personality in order to gain an insight into how he plays. The more information you can ascertain about his play, the more likely you will be able to make an educated guess as to what type of hand he is holding. With that knowledge you gain a tremendous advantage. Poker is not solitaire; you ignore your opponents' playing style at your own peril.

In business negotiations, it is equally important to know both yourself and your opponent. First, you must know your limit and stick to it. We have all been done in by a slick salesman or adversary who convinced us to pay more than we wanted to for something. That's why it is important to set realistic goals ahead of time and to stick to your guns whether you are negotiating for your company or yourself. However, this is only half the equation. You must also know your opponent's limits if you are going to get the best deal possible. You are much better off paying your adversary's minimum price than your maximum price. Your company will thank you for it. And if it's for yourself, you'll obviously benefit.

For example, say you are looking to buy a new car. You have done your research and you have set a maximum price of $24,500 that you are willing to pay. The dealer has a minimum price at which it is willing to sell. That price is $23,250. If you walk into that dealership, hoping to get as low a price as possible but are willing to pay $24,500, I guarantee you will end up paying $24,500. However, if you go to that same dealership with the primary goal of finding out how low the dealer will go, I guarantee that you will end up paying less than $24,500, and, hopefully, a lot closer to $23,250 than $24,500. In the first example, you're playing solitaire. In the second, you are playing poker.

Poker is a game of interaction. Take the time to test and probe the salesperson. Know the markup of both the car and any extras the dealer may have added, such as pinstripes or mud flaps. Talk to other dealers. Find out about the dealer incentives. Inquire about personal incentives for salespeople. Gain as much information as possible in order to put the salesperson "on a hand." If it's the end of the month and the salesperson needs one or two more car sales to be the leading salesperson that month, then it may be worthwhile for him to take less of a commission on this sale in order to qualify for a potentially bigger bonus. Finally, be willing to walk away. You can always come back the next day.

There is another reason to know your opponent as best as you can.

Not every situation need be purely adversarial. In fact, there are plenty of opportunities to create win-win situations for all involved, if you make the effort to understand the other side. For instance, say you make an offer for a house and the seller comes back and says she has received another offer for the same price. Rather than upping your bid, find out what else is important to the seller. If the seller is moving to new construction, she may need flexibility with her settlement date. If you can help her out in this regard and keep her from having to move twice, that may be more valuable to her than increasing your offer by $2,000.

If you do not take the time and make the effort to know the other side, then you cannot effectively make the best deal for yourself. Whether you are playing poker or negotiating a contract, the more you know about the other person, the more successful you will be.

MAKE A PLAY FOR THE POT

In poker, the first person to bet at the pot often wins it. Players who make a play for the pot put their opponent on the defensive. There is a tremendous tactical advantage to taking the offensive. This does not mean betting at every pot. That is a reckless and transparent strategy that will only cost you a lot of money. However, experienced players will judiciously pick and choose opportune times to play and then take the offensive.

Taking the offensive gives a player more opportunities to win. You can win by having the best hand or you can win by chasing your opponent out. For example, say you started with ace-king and the flop comes eight-nine-two with two hearts. Neither of your cards is a heart. You make a big bet after the flop and get called by one opponent. By betting big, you project strength to your opponents. If you continue to bet or raise, it may not matter if you improve. If your opponents do not improve, they are likely to fold their hand. Now, if the turn brings a card such as the four of clubs, you stand an excellent chance of taking down the pot by making a big bet. If your opponent is on a straight or flush draw, he should now fold. Even if he has a hand such as ten-nine giving him top pair, he may have a hard time calling, since your betting action suggests you started holding a high pair.

If instead of taking the offensive with this hand, however, you decide to check to see what your opponent does, the dynamics completely change. Now, if your opponent bets and you call, hoping to improve, you have lost your leverage. If your hand does not improve, you will most likely fold. You empower your opponent by letting him control the betting. He gains confidence and is unlikely to believe that you have a strong hand. By calling his bets you gain nothing. So even though you commit the same amount of money in both situations, you stand a much better chance of success when you take the offensive.

Apply this strategy in negotiating. When that car salesman asks what you want your monthly payment to be, answer that it depends on a number of factors. Then take the offensive. Ask if there are any rebates or interest rate specials. Let him reveal any offers that are available. Then begin to negotiate from there. Negotiate each item individually. Negotiate a purchase price first. Then insist on a favorable interest rate. If you do not get what you perceive to be a favorable rate, let the salesman know that you will work with your own bank. Lastly, negotiate the trade-in.

During all aspects of the negotiation, take the offensive. Be the one to ask the questions. Put the salesman on the defensive. Probe him for answers so he reveals information to you.

Another reason to take the offensive is to gain information. When you put your opponent on the defensive how he reacts is revealing. In poker, if a player raises you after you have taken the offensive, you can probably put him on a hand stronger than yours. You have now gained information and you can act accordingly. Similarly, when you take the offensive in any negotiation, you can gain information from the other party's reaction. If you are insisting on a low price from the car salesman and he is willing to let you walk away rather than give into the price, you have gained information as to the strength of his bargaining position. Perhaps you are shopping for a super hot model that they cannot keep in stock. In any event, the more information you gain by taking the offensive can only help you in reaching an informed decision.

Say you are buying materials for a new product your company is making. You know that projections for this product are through the roof. Even so, you still have limited authority for how much you can order now. In the negotiations, even though you can't commit to large minimum quantities, there are other ways to get the point across. Rather than make an empty promise along the lines of "If this thing takes off, we'll be ordering a ton more," try a different tactic. Statements like that ring hollow, and vendors have heard them all before. Instead, express your concern that a major issue for you is the vendor's capacity. Let the vendor know that you are only going to go with someone who can meet your anticipated needs down the road, and let him know what those needs will likely be. This statement will ring true.

DO NOT ACT UNTIL IT IS YOUR TURN TO ACT

In poker, players should never act until it is their turn to act. That is, every player should check, bet, raise, or fold in turn. As simple as this concept is, it is amazing how many beginning players (and even some experienced players) routinely ignore it. Every time I play, some player will throw her cards in before it is her turn to act. This is obviously in bad form and can influence a player who has yet to act, but it is also harmful to the player who does it. Why is it harmful to the player who folds early if he was going to fold anyway? Because there will be times when a player should play a hand, depending on what those in front of him do. In Hold 'em, position is of the utmost importance. A player in late position has an advantage in being able to see how everyone else acts before his turn (except for the blinds, who have forced bets). A player in late position can play some marginal hands, if everyone in front of him folds. A poker player should never make an ultimate decision until he has all the available information to do so. By waiting until it is your turn to act, you have the benefit of knowing what those before you have done before you make a decision.

Yet, I often see a player (let's call him Player Careless) in late position look at his cards and then pick them up, and it is blatantly obvious that he is just waiting until it is his turn to fold. Even if Player Careless waits for his turn to toss in his cards, he has already announced to the table that he is going to fold. This may allow the player in front of Player Careless to bet, knowing that Player Careless is going to fold. In the event everyone does fold to Player Careless, Player Careless has now blown any chance to take advantage of his position. If the other players have been paying attention, they know that Player Careless does not have a strong hand.

In everyday life, be careful not to jump the gun. Wait until it is your turn to act so you have the advantage of knowing every bit of available information. Listening is an extremely valuable tool in negotiating. If the other guy wants to talk, let him. Hear him out, as he may offer some clues to his position. You'll get your chance to speak. I have witnessed opposing parties at a business meeting speak over each other many times to the point where one party is still negotiating a point that the other has conceded. If she only took the time to listen, she would be in a better position to further her own cause and career. When someone is articulating an argument, listen carefully and even jot down notes if you need to. When it's your turn to speak, you will be able to construct your argument to best counter what you just heard.

No matter what you are negotiating, if you make an offer that is rejected, wait for a counteroffer. Do not be careless or overanxious. Wait for a reply so you have all of the available information. It's his turn to act, so let him. Don't jump the gun. Otherwise, you are bidding against yourself and playing into the other party's hand.

FIND AN EDGE

In poker, you either find an edge or you lose money. You must outwit, outwork, and out-will your opponents. Even then you may not find an edge; poker forces you to be resourceful. The good player will find a weakness in his opponent's game to exploit. When things are rough, the good player will use position or the power of his chip stack to create an edge. He will attack an opponent when he is vulnerable, regardless of what cards the good player is holding.

I highly encourage every poker player to play in a tournament on a regular basis. Even if players do not like tournament play or find them unprofitable, playing in a tournament can greatly enhance their overall game. The structure of tournaments forces players to become resourceful. Every tournament participant but one will be eliminated. Unlike regular poker games, everyone starts with the same number of chips in a tournament, and the blinds/antes and betting amounts increase at regular intervals. Thus, players cannot afford to wait for perfect cards. Players must find an edge or their chip stacks will dwindle away and they will be eliminated.

Find that edge in negotiations. If you want to get ahead, you should always be willing to outwork, outwit, and out-will everyone else. That may not always be enough, however. Be resourceful and creative to find an edge. During negotiations, look for a weakness in your adversary to exploit. I can remember working on the sale of a significant corporation during my first year out of law school. Our negotiations with the buyer toward a definitive acquisition agreement started on a Friday afternoon and continued straight through to Sunday afternoon with only one four-hour break in the wee hours Saturday morning. As you can imagine, these transactions are heavily staffed. As a first-year attorney, I was close to the bottom of the totem pole. Since the negotiations were taking place at our offices, my duties included proofreading documents, running back and forth to the copy room, and ordering food. Since there were two teams of attorneys, investment bankers, and businesspeople working around the clock, I was ordering plenty of food—breakfast, lunch, dinner, and midnight snacks. After Sunday morning's breakfast of bagels and fruit, the partner in charge (let's call him Mr. A) pulled all of the junior attorneys and paralegals aside and stated that the next person to order food would be fired (after the deal was consummated, of course).

I learned a lesson that I will never forget. Mr. A was trying to create an edge for our client. He wanted to force the other side's hand and he did not want any more distractions or breaks. While there were other potential buyers, the seller greatly preferred this buyer, and Mr. A had set a Sunday evening deadline to get a deal in place before we would talk to the other potential buyers. Mr. A knew that if Sunday's deadline came and went, we would lose all leverage with this potential buyer if we continued negotiations or came back to the buyer at a later date. Of course, by late Sunday evening, as the parties fought hunger and exhaustion, the negotiations progressed quickly and a contract was signed. Mr. A had effectively turned the negotiations from a regular poker game into a tournament.

Force yourself to be resourceful. If negotiations are stalled, consider creating an artificial deadline to move things along. Think of alternatives to the transaction. We sometimes get so consumed with negotiations that getting the deal done at any cost becomes the end game. If you can live with not doing the deal, then you create some breathing room and give yourself space. If you decide to continue negotiations, you will now have an edge, knowing that you can walk away at any time and be content with that result.

BE THE RULER OF YOUR TABLE

When you play within your means, you play with confidence. You can afford to take charge. The poker player who takes charge of his table is a successful poker player. How do you take charge of your table? By sensing and attacking weakness in your opponent, by taking advantage of position to gain an edge over your opponent, by betting aggressively whenever you perceive an advantage, and, finally and most important, by dictating the terms of play.

Being the ruler of the table requires decisive, aggressive action. If you are going to play a hand, be the one to bet out or raise. That shows strength. Avoid checking and calling. That displays weakness. Good players are consistent and firm in their actions. They do not play recklessly yet they very reluctantly give up their dominance. They do not give their opponents any opportunity to be the aggressor. When you play with strength, you will soon find that your opponents are adjusting their play to yours. They are less likely to enter pots that you are in. They are less likely to bet into you knowing you may raise. When opponents conform their play to yours, you have a tremendous advantage. Now, not only will you win the pots when you have strong cards, you will win the pots when your opponent is vulnerable, even if you don't have a strong hand either. And when your opponents do have a strong hand, you will know it by the way they fight back instead of following your lead.

In any negotiation you enter, you must be the one to establish the boundaries. If you leave your opponents with an opening, they will jump through it. You must assume that they have the tenacity of a maniac poker player who will keep firing chips into the pot until someone stops him. They will push you to the limit. That is why you must take control of the negotiations. You must be the one to dictate the terms of play. You must be the ruler of the table.

How many times have you been in negotiation and the other party has said to you, "Don't nickel and dime me!"? What was your response? Did you let the point go? Well, you shouldn't. Those are your nickels and dimes we are talking about, and you are entitled to them. Furthermore, it is usually not nickels and dimes, either. For instance, say you are looking at buying a new car. You have agreed to a price on the car and now you are haggling over the value of your old car that you want to trade in. You have done your research, and the dealer is only willing to go to a price that is still $250 below your last offer. You offer to split the difference—which would mean the dealer would come up another $125. The dealer says, "Don't nickel and dime me." Well, since the new car you are buying is over $25,000, that $125 seems relatively insignificant in this context. That is exactly what the dealer is hoping you think. However, $125 is still One Hundred and Twenty-Five Dollars. That is money in your pocket. If you took that same car to get washed and the car wash tried to charge you an extra $125, you would never pay it. You would have no problem being the ruler of the table in that situation. While context is important, do not be blinded by it. The ruler of the table never is.

We've all heard the saying that "a lawyer who represents himself has a fool for a client." That's because the lawyer's judgment may be impaired when he is so personally involved. The person who wants a deal the most is often at a disadvantage. If you and your co-workers are in negotiations with another company, try to determine who wants to get the deal done the most—on both your side and the other side. Direct your comments to the identified person on the other side and try to keep the counterpart on your side out of the direct negotiations.

BE AN OPEN-MINDED DICTATOR

In poker, the bottom line is to win. You are measured by how much money you are up or down. Establishing yourself as the ruler of the table will go a long way toward helping you win. However, a good player does not become so consumed with trying to establish her dominance that she forgets the bottom line. A good player does not attempt to be a dictator at all costs. That is a losing proposition. There will be times when the cards are running really bad for you. A good player will ease up and try to cut her losses. There will be times when you are playing with really weak, loose players who call every hand to the end. In this situation, a good player will be less concerned about establishing her dominance and will just wait for a good hand to play, since she knows these weak players will eventually pay her off. There will be times when you are up against a stronger opponent or an opponent who is just making all the right moves against you that day. A good player will recognize this and either take a break or leave the table altogether for another game. Being the ruler of the table does not mean throwing common sense out the window. Good players do not crave power for the sake of power. Rather, they desire to ascend to power in order to control the table and become profitable. If you run into difficulty at the poker table trying to establish your dominance, or if there is a better way to make money at the table, good players adapt. Good players are flexible and do what is best for their bankroll.

In both the poker room and my professional career, I have had the opportunity to observe countless people of varying personalities. I have both witnessed and negotiated against the very best lawyers and businesspeople. I have witnessed and played against the very best poker players. On the other hand, I have come across some pretty poor lawyers, businesspeople, and poker players. I have crossed paths, and tangled, with all types. Of all these types, I find that the easiest personality to go up against are the ones who desire power for the sake of power. They have an easily identifiable Achilles' heel—their massive ego. They are more interested in establishing their power than winning. In poker, these types will gladly raise and re-raise and give you their money rather than fold. They want you to know that they will bet that pot no matter what. They are more concerned with controlling the table than winning. So how do you play against this type? You wait for a good hand and let Mr. Ego give you his money.

In negotiations, these types are more interested in showing everyone in the conference room that they are smarter, tougher, and more powerful than anyone else. How do you negotiate against this type? You stroke his ego and let him look good in front of his clients. Fight like heck on points you do not care about. Turn these inconsequential points into major issues, so when you let Mr. Ego win he will feel mighty and powerful. Low-key the more important issues. Do not make him contentious. Remember, Mr. Ego would rather win arguments than points. He is more concerned with establishing his power than negotiating a good deal. Take advantage of that. Be open-minded and adjust your strategy. Control the negotiation in a more subtle way. Be an open-minded dictator.

BE A BENEVOLENT DICTATOR

No one likes to feel that she is existing under a dictator. In poker, good players want to control the action and their opponents, but they do not want their opponents to feel oppressed. A good poker player will attack his opponent's weaknesses, rattle his opponent's confidence, and establish his dominance over his opponent. However, he will also try to keep his opponent happy. Most losing players view poker purely as a recreational activity. They set aside a certain amount of discretionary income to play, and while they would like to win, it is more important to them that they have a good time. Experienced poker players recognize this and feed into it. A good poker player encourages his weak opponents even when that opponent beats him. For instance, take the situation where the good poker player (let's call him Mr. Pro) is an overwhelming favorite in a hand against a weak recreational player whom we will call Mr. Tourist. Mr. Pro bets every step of the way, knowing that Mr. Tourist will call any bet, hoping to catch a miracle card. Well, on the last card, Mr. Tourist happens to catch one of the only two cards left in the deck that could help him, so Mr. Tourist beats Mr. Pro. Mr. Pro, if he is smart, will congratulate Mr. Tourist on his tough, smart play. Why would Mr. Pro do this? Because nine times out of ten, Mr. Tourist will lose that hand and Mr. Pro will make money. Mr. Pro recognizes this and therefore he encourages Mr. Tourist's wasteful behavior.

Yet time and time again, I witness very experienced poker players (let's call one of them Mr. Belligerent) berate others for their poor play—even when Mr. Belligerent wins. Mr. Belligerent just cannot help himself. He feels compelled to point out every mistake Mr. Tourist makes. He makes Mr. Tourist feel lousy about himself. For example, take a situation where Mr. Tourist calls Mr. Belligerent's bets when Mr. Tourist clearly has the worst hand. As Mr. Belligerent scoops the pot, he points out Mr. Tourist's obvious mistake to the rest of the table. What Mr. Belligerent should be doing is telling Mr. Tourist what a tough opponent he is and how Mr. Belligerent would have played Mr. Tourist's hand exactly the same way. Instead, if Mr. Belligerent continues to criticize Mr. Tourist's play, one of two things will likely happen. Mr. Tourist will get up and leave the table and find another table where he can lose his money or Mr. Tourist will start playing better and attacking Mr. Belligerent. If Mr. Belligerent could just find it within himself to be civil to Mr. Tourist, Mr. Belligerent would be the beneficiary of Mr. Tourist's poor play. Instead, Mr. Tourist will either fight back or move on to another table where there will be players more than willing to befriend him.

Everyone likes respect. In any negotiation you enter into in life, it is worthwhile to keep things civil. It is to your benefit. You are trying to control the negotiations in order to win points and get a favorable deal or produce a favorable outcome. You are much more likely to accomplish this if you are courteous and respectful to the other side. People like to feel good about themselves. If you insist on berating or belittling the other side, one of two things are likely to happen. Either they will get much tougher in their negotiations or they will walk away and deal with someone else. If you behave this way at your own company, people will work around you.

While you want to dictate the terms of play, you also want to keep people engaged and contented. It is a fine balancing act you must accomplish in order to take control of the negotiations while keeping everyone involved happy. Be a benevolent dictator.

KNOW WHAT IS MATERIAL TO YOUR OPPONENT

I see too many poker players make the following mistake. We will use Player A as an example. Player A is playing in a no-limit Hold 'em tournament and wants to chase an opponent out of a pot. That opponent has a fairly large chip stack. Player A makes a bet that represents a pretty sizable amount of Player A's stack. It is a large enough bet that Player A would have a hard time calling such a bet if his opponent had bet it. The trouble is that the amount bet is not that large in relation to the opponent's stack. In fact, the opponent has no problem making the call. Player A's fundamental mistake here is not considering what would be a significant bet for his opponent to call. Player A is guilty of only thinking in terms of what would be material to him. Big mistake.

In any negotiation, try to determine what is material to your opponent. Say you are about to make an offer on a house and you know that the seller really needs to close quickly, as she is buying another home. You are flexible, since you are on a month-to-month lease and may even prefer to close sooner as opposed to later. *Do not just give the point up, though, because it is not material to you.* Use that information to your advantage. Let the seller know that you would really like to close later but you will try to work out something in order to help her. Trade moving the closing date up for something you want.

By knowing what is material to the seller, you can effectively negotiate concessions. If you only concentrate on what is material to you, you make the negotiations that much more difficult. You have no leverage. You are negotiating from weakness. Negotiate from strength. Determine what is material to your opponent and make that your starting point.

Do Not Reveal Your Hand When You Are Not Called

Typically in poker, if you make a big bet and your opponent folds, then you quietly throw your cards face down to the dealer without showing anyone what you had. Or, say you call an opponent on the river because you are not quite sure that he has the flush that he is representing and you are hoping that your two pair is good. Sure enough, he has the flush. Again, the correct move is to muck your cards. Mucking your cards means discarding your cards without revealing them. As simple and elementary as this principle is, it is amazing how many players violate it. While there is the rare occasion when you want to reveal your hand to set your up opponent for a later move, most of the time a player reveals his hand for one reason only—his ego. He wants to show his opponents that he successfully bluffed a player out of a pot. Or he wants to show that he had a decent, albeit losing, hand when he called the bet at the end.

This player lets his ego get the best of him. The more information your opponents can gather on you, the better they can play against you. Yet some players just cannot help themselves. They choose to massage their own egos, even if that helps opponents get a read on them.

Never reveal your hand when you don't have to. As noted earlier, I have witnessed many lawyers, investment bankers, and business-people argue points that the other side has already conceded. Why do they do this? I can only guess that their egos gets the best of them. They feel the need to show everyone in the conference room how smart they are. In the case of lawyers and investment bankers, maybe they want to impress their clients. However, revealing their hand when they do not have to is counterproductive. The other side now has a read on them. They have needlessly antagonized the other side and have most likely made further negotiations more difficult. The other side will now think twice about conceding future points even for issues that are not that important to them. By trying to show off to their clients, they have hurt their clients' negotiating position. At the end of the day, clients will see right through this.

Early on in my career, I was fortunate to have as a mentor a senior partner who never felt the need to argue a point when he did not have to. If opposing counsel conceded a point, he would acknowledge the fairness of that position and move on quickly. By keeping opposing counsel in a conciliatory mood, he would extract the best deal for his clients without needless bluster. Clients can see through bluster.

Bluster is revealing your hand. To put things in perspective, at the end of more deals than I can count, the oppositions' clients would approach my mentor, seeking his representation for future work. That is the highest compliment a professional can receive.

PROJECT THE RIGHT TABLE IMAGE

Image counts for a lot at the poker table. Those players who show confidence and strength will succeed. Opposing players will conform their play to the strong player. If you are strong at the poker table, opponents will hesitate entering into pots with you. They will avoid betting into you. They will not want to act, knowing you are yet to act behind them. In short, they will not be able to play their game. Every move they make will be made with you in mind. By projecting the right table image, you will control both your opponents and the action at the table.

Take control of your everyday negotiations. Never show weakness. Project strength and confidence in order to throw the other party off of her game. Let your adversaries conform their actions to yours. You control the action.

Many negotiations have multiple parties on both sides. It's critical to make sure that you caucus with everyone on your side ahead of time, be it co-workers, attorneys, accountants, and so on. If you are going to show strength, you must be united and on the same page. Often, the person who is closest to the negotiation (i.e., reaching a resolution is most important to them) will be the person to show the first signs of weakness. It's a good idea to have her take a backseat in the negotiations. Try to have one unifying force communicated by one leader and backed up by the others.

Dissent is never fruitful. You never want to be in a position of having to negotiate with your own people in front of the other side. The parameters should be set ahead of time that if anyone does feel differently, they should wait until a break to discuss it privately. At that time, that person should be allowed to be heard completely. Often that difference can be used effectively in a good cop/bad cop scenario. Those situations should be well thought out and not done spontaneously.

By projecting the right table image, you can control not only the negotiations but the subsequent performance, which is even more critical. For example, if you are negotiating with a contractor to finish your basement, have him come to your house at a time that allows you to focus and concentrate your full energy on the task at hand. Be specific about what you want and your expectations. Have a game plan set out beforehand and stick to it. Be confident about both your desires and expectations. Make it clear that you are knowledgeable about both construction and its pricing.

While the contractor is sure to have helpful suggestions, remember that it is your house and basement. Be firm. You can still be polite, but do not feel any pressure to take a suggestion that you are not sold on. If you set the tone from the outset, the contractor will learn quickly to drop ideas that you reject. If you make it clear from the beginning that you expect quality workmanship, the contractor will be less likely to take shortcuts. If you make it clear that payment will based on certain milestones being achieved in a timely fashion, there will be little chance for delays.

By projecting the right image, you are controlling the action. Show confidence and strength to get the efficient and quality job that you deserve and are paying for.

DO NOT GIVE YOUR OPPONENT FREE CARDS

The one mistake weak, inexperienced players make time and again is to give their opponents free cards. In poker, whenever you have the best hand, you need to bet it. Otherwise, you offer your opponents the opportunity to draw more cards in order to beat you. If your opponent wants to draw cards to try to beat you, make him pay for it. If you were playing football and the game ended with your team ahead by four points and the opposing team on your five-yard line, you would take the victory and run into the locker room. You certainly would not offer the opposing team another couple of minutes to try to beat you. As simple as that concept sounds, it is amazing how many poker players will give their opponents that very opportunity. They will put time on the clock for them. If you have a poker hand that is the best hand but beatable, you have to bet. You simply cannot afford to give your opponents free cards and allow them to beat you.

Do not give free cards in your negotiations. If you are negotiating and you have successfully won a few key points, do not think that you owe the other side one. Remain a strong advocate for your positions. If you need to trade one issue for another in order to compromise, then by all means do it. However, never feel that you have to sacrifice an issue because you have won more than the other side.

Never give up leverage. If you have any edge, you must use it to your advantage. To do otherwise is to give your opponent a free card. Again, if you are shopping for a car at the end of the month and you know your salesman needs only a couple more sales to reach monthly incentives, then press hard for the best deal. This salesman may gain a lot in incentives even if he takes no commission on the sale to you. In a few days, however, your leverage may be gone. Use it to your full advantage while you have it.

If you are looking to buy a new house and you do not have one to sell, that is a key factor in your favor. Use it to your advantage. Let the seller know that you do not need a sale contingency. If the seller replies that that is not worth anything to him, then call him on it. Try to stretch the closing out and see how he reacts. Ask for an aggressive mortgage rate contingency and see how he responds. Test him to see if he is just trying to get a free card or if your lack of a sale contingency is really worth something.

Do not be quick to dismiss any perceived advantage that you may have. Everyone likes to get free cards when they have a drawing hand. They will feign strength in the hopes that you will not force their hand

and that you will let them see another card for free. Do not give them those free cards. When you have leverage, use it. Make your adversaries pay for those extra cards.

DO NOT BE A CALLING STATION

Experienced poker players love to play against calling stations. Calling stations are weak, loose players. A calling station never met a hand he did not like. He is the eternal optimist at the poker table. He believes every hand has potential and he will play it no matter how long the odds are that his hand will improve to become a winning one. The calling station will call any bet until the river. If he does not make his hand on the river, he will fold. To hasten his demise, the calling station will never take the lead in betting unless he has a real strong hand.

The calling station is an ideal opponent because he lets others control the betting. If you have a strong hand, the calling station is sure to pay you off. Even if you are on a draw and miss making your hand, you can likely force the calling station to fold (assuming he missed his as well) by betting aggressively on the river. Finally, if a calling station does have a strong hand, you will know it (since it will be the only time he takes the lead in betting) and you can save a lot of money by folding.

Do not be a calling station in negotiations. Stand up for yourself. Be proactive. Calling stations let others dictate the terms. In negotiations, the calling station is way too agreeable. He is passive and willing to agree to any terms unless he feels very strongly to the contrary. If you're up against one in negotiations, keep the atmosphere light and jovial and win every point.

THE POKER EXPERIENCE

Liar's Poker

Working as an attorney on Wall Street, we kept some crazy hours. There were many all-nighters and plenty of ninety-plus–hour work-weeks. There would be downtime in between deals and other periods where we were waiting on the word processing department to finish a long document. A favorite pastime of the younger attorneys to break the stress and bide the down time was to play liar's poker.

To play liar's poker, everyone took out a few dollar bills from their pockets and piled them up in front of them without looking at the serial numbers. Each player would then pick up one dollar bill to "play with." Every dollar bill has eight numbers that make up the serial number. Those numbers represented each player's cards. For example, I just took a dollar bill out of my pocket, and the serial number is D47942749B. You ignore the letters, so my hand is 47942749. To simplify, I rearrange the number and I have 444, 99, 77, 2. What's different about liar's poker, though, is that you are playing everyone's numbers collectively, not just your own hand.

Say we have eight players. With eight serial numbers per bill, that's a total of sixty-four numbers in play. With ten potential numbers (0–9), on average there will be 6.4 of each number. Of course, due to the randomization of the numbers, there will be more of some numbers than others. Since I have three fours, I am in a good position to guess that there are more than the average number of fours out there. How I use that information, though, is key. One person will start the bid-ding, and he can start with as low as one zero or he can say as high a number as he wants. The action then moves clockwise in a circle, and each succeeding player must either state a higher number or call. For instance, say the first player starts out by stating three sixes. The next player must state at least three sevens or higher. He could state four twos or even eight sixes, as long as his number is higher than three sixes.

The action ends when one player finally calls. Say after a few rounds of bidding, the action gets to me, and the last person to act says eleven threes following a flurry of bidding on threes. I could take a chance and say eleven fours, since I have three of them. Or I could say twelve threes if I think that there really are a lot of threes out there even though I don't have any. Or I could call. If I call, then everyone turns over their bills and we count up the threes. If there are at least eleven threes, I lose and I must pay everyone a dollar. If there are not eleven threes, then the player who bid eleven threes loses and he must pay everyone a dollar. The key to success in this game is to not be either the player calling or the player called. That way, you win no matter what.

At some point in the game, however, you are going to reach a critical point where it becomes just as risky to bid a higher number as it does to call. There is a lot of strategy involved. For instance, say it's my turn and the bid is only three eights. I can immediately jump to seven fours. Since seven of one number is unlikely to be called in an eight-person game, I am relatively safe. Even if I am called, I stand a good chance of winning, holding three fours. Finally, by ratcheting up the bidding, the action is unlikely to make it all the way around to me another time.

What I like most about this game is that, unlike regular poker, there is no checking or folding option. All will be put to the test at some point and they must either decide to raise or call. All players are forced to make tough decisions. You must be able to read everyone else in the game in order to optimize your decision-making process. It's a great tool to practice negotiating techniques. At times you are working with other players and at times you are working against them. At times you are trying to lead players in a certain direction and at times you are trying to test them. And at times, you will be put to the test. There is no folding in negotiation. When put to the test, you must be creative, confident, and unwavering in your response.

5. BLUFF OR FOLD: EFFECTIVE NEGOTIATING NO MATTER WHAT HAND YOU ARE DEALT

To make correct decisions in poker, it's best to concentrate on the process and not worry about the end result. Study your opponents, keep abreast of their moves, and make adjustments. Do those things consistently and you will be in a position to make correct decisions, and success will likely follow. Sometimes, despite our best intentions, it's tough to keep our focus on the process. If a loud, obnoxious player sits down and plays aggressively, your whole process can be thrown off. Many of these players appear to be loose and out of control, when, in fact, their act is well orchestrated to create maximum confusion. The key to their success is to disrupt everyone else's thought processes.

Playing against these types of players can be challenging. A fine balancing act between adjusting to their style and keeping focused on your own process is required. By "process," I mean sticking to your game and making correct decisions based on the totality of circumstances. You cannot let these players run amok over the table, yet you cannot completely buy into their game, either. If one of these maniacs insists on raising the stakes every hand, you're going to have to take a stand at some point. You have to select situations to fight back to slow these players down so you can regain control over your process.

Your process is just as important at the negotiating table as it is at the poker table. If you can concentrate on the process and on making correct decisions, the desired results will likely follow. If you allow someone else to disrupt that process, you are at a disadvantage. Law firms are notorious for wanting that home court advantage. A good lawyer will typically insist on drafting the key documents for his client. By doing so, he can artfully craft language in his favor. Often, there might be agreement on the larger issues, but creative draftsmanship can offer subtle but significant differences. In a big acquisition agreement, you can imagine all of the nuances that must be covered in a host of different areas. These documents can be lengthy, and modifying terms like *reasonable* and *material* can significantly alter meaning and liability. By controlling the process, a good lawyer can drastically bend the bias toward his client.

Of course, the lawyer for the opposing side is not helpless. She will try to wrestle control away. Instead of offering comments or suggestions, she will revise the document herself and offer in return a new document that tracks her changes. To prevent this, the original lawyer may fax a copy instead of e-mailing the document, which easily allows for the other side to put the document on their system and make changes. A lot of effort goes into controlling the process because the end result is often more favorable to the side that does so. It's much easier to insert a favorable position when drafting a document than to convince the other side to insert it for you.

Controlling the process is power. Car dealerships are adept at doing this. Step onto a lot, and a salesperson will greet you within seconds. He will be extremely gracious, courteous, and accommodating. Any car you want to see, he'll let you test ride and point out all of its great features. He'll establish a rapport and a trust. As soon as you show interest in striking a deal, however, what happens?

You'll be escorted to a tiny little waiting room and asked to have a seat. Or you may have a seat at the salesperson's desk. Any negotiation on your part will usually require approval of the manager. Of course, the manager is never readily available, and you never get to speak with her yourself. Rather, you are left to wait on their turf while the salesperson disappears for quite some time. After about twenty minutes, the salesperson will finally come back with a minor concession that is nowhere near what you want. This may go back and forth for quite some time before the manager herself magically appears. She will make what she characterizes as her final offer, which is only good right now, because they have some extra incentive from the manufacturer to more sales done before the end of the month. It doesn't matter that it's the eleventh day of the month. Today is when their "fiscal month ends," she informs you.

This is all part of the process of the dealership. They know that the longer things drag out and the more time and effort a customer invests there, the more chance of his eventually weakening. If you were in the comfort of your home negotiating by telephone, it would be a lot easier to say no. You wouldn't have to wait around for a reply to your negotiations. You could simply ask them to call you back. Being refreshed, energized, and comfortable sure beats being tired, hungry, and uncomfortable in a crowded dealership. Good luck, however, trying to get a quote on the telephone from a car dealership.

To counteract these tactics, you have to come up with a way to regain control of the process. Don't play their game. If you're kept waiting too long, start to walk out. Someone will stop you before you leave. Insist on an answer or ask for a business card. Tell them to call you at home with a reply. If they make an offer, tell them you'll think about it and call them back. They need you more than you need them. You don't have to buy a car from them. If they lose you, they lose a sale. It's a situation where the customer should control the process but rarely docs.

Think about the process of whatever negotiations you are entering ahead of time and how you can maintain control. Arrange for meetings in your offices or home if it is feasible. Be sure to eat a light meal ahead of time so you don't get hungry or weak. Insist on your attorney drafting the documents. It may be a little more expensive, but you'll end up with a better deal. Stick to the issues of your concern. If you're up against a maniac who likes to yell and argue a lot, don't play his game. Remain calm and focused and keep the conversation objective and businesslike. Don't allow an aggressive opponent to run amok at the negotiating table. If you can't settle him down, then suggest corresponding via e-mail or through an intermediary. Find an alternative that allows you to reestablish the process that will satisfy your needs.

Mix Up Your Play so You Are Not Predictable

If you gain an advantage by understanding your opponent, then it follows that your opponent will gain an advantage by understanding you. If you cannot make the best deal for yourself without knowledge of your opponent, then your opponent cannot make the best deal for himself without knowledge of you. In poker, one prevents this by mixing up his play to keep his game from becoming predictable. You do not want your opponent to put you on a hand.

When you walk into that car dealership, you do not want the salesperson to know your maximum price. In fact, you may not even want him to know how serious you are about buying a car. Let him know that you are considering other options. Mention competing models that are priced more affordably. Talk about features that other cars have that this one is missing. Do not feel compelled to work with whatever salesman first approaches you if you are not comfortable with him. Visit a few times. See which cars are still on the lot and which cars are moving. Mix up your play. Be enthusiastic one visit and disinterested the next. Find out what works the best.

Do Not Force the Action

No matter how much you study and analyze your opponent, there will be plenty of times when you cannot put him on a hand. An experienced poker player will be mixing up his play just as you should be mixing up yours. When you cannot get a good read on a player, do not force the action. You do not want to bet into a situation when you do not have adequate information. This can be very dangerous. An opposing player may be trapping you. In other words, he wants you to bet into him because he knows he has you beat. He is feigning weakness hoping you will gain a false sense of confidence.

When you enter into a negotiation, do not be so determined to close a deal that you back yourself into a corner. If you do not have adequate information, then do not force the action. If you are in a car dealership, then by definition you will be negotiating with someone who has exponentially more experience than you do in negotiating cars. You are going to buy a new car every few years at most. Which means you will be negotiating once every few years. That salesman you are negotiating with negotiates dozens of deals a week. It will be extremely difficult to gain information from him. He knows every trick in the book. He will effectively mix up his play. He will deliberately try to trap you. Do not bet into him.

How do you accomplish this? Do not volunteer information. Make him give you a price first. If you are not satisfied, rather than make a counteroffer, tell him you are not in the same ballpark. If you are financing the car, do not let him know what you are willing to pay on a monthly basis. Negotiate the price of the car first and then negotiate financing. Do not let him back you into a payment that lets you think you are getting a good price on the car when you are, in fact, paying a higher-than-market interest rate. Again, be willing to walk away.

A common mistake of beginning poker players is to stay in a pot when they feel they have too much committed. That is, once they have a few bets in the pot, they feel they have too much invested, so they end up throwing more money into the pot with a losing hand rather than folding. Whenever you are negotiating, leave yourself an out. It is never too late to back out of a negotiation. If you find that you are committing more than you should, call it off. Do not feel that you have invested too much time to walk away, even if you have been negotiating for hours. If you do not like the way the negotiations are going and you feel you may end up with a losing deal, then fold and walk away. Just like it is never too late to fold a losing poker hand, it is never too late to walk away from a losing negotiation.

NEVER TIP YOUR HAND

One of the most elementary concepts in poker and in life is to never tip your hand. In poker, the more information you can hide from your opponent, the better. Thus, if your opponent can guess what you are holding, he has a big advantage. That is why poker players go to great lengths to avoid giving tells. You see players wearing ten-gallon hats, oversized sunglasses, and anything else they can find that they believe will hide their emotions. They do not want to tip their hand. On the other hand, you will find players staring down their opponents and asking questions, hoping to pick up some information. Players are consistently trying to hide the value of their own hand while trying to ascertain what their opponents may be holding.

While this interplay is obvious in poker, such situations in real life can range from the obvious to the subtle. On the obvious side, we all know to conceal our excitement when walking through a house that we love and want to bid on. However, just as some poker players cannot hide their hands, some folks just cannot hide their excitement in the presence of the sellers. If you are not capable of a poker face, try to have your agent show you properties when the sellers are not home. Be aware, however, that even an agent representing you will want to make a deal. You must be careful to keep your enthusiasm to yourself.

Car salesmen are notorious for trying to gain information from prospective buyers. A favorite trick is to ask customers what they want their monthly payments to be. Many unsuspecting customers answer this question, not sensing any harm in doing so. Big mistake. They are tipping their hand. They are giving away information that they do not need to give. Monthly payments are a function of many factors, including total purchase price, down payment, interest rate, and, if applicable, the value of a trade-in. Each of these should be negotiated separately. However, an unsuspecting buyer who volunteers information allows the salesman to back into the number. The salesman is now free to manipulate any of the factors above to arrive at a monthly payment within your range. If he senses you are dead-set on paying only a $1,000 above invoice, he will charge a higher interest rate or lowball you on the trade.

In any negotiation or situation where your interests are not aligned with the other party, do not volunteer any unnecessary information. Do not tip your hand. Disclose information on a "need to know" basis only.

TELL A CONSISTENT STORY

When you are playing poker, every hand tells a story. If you are paying attention, you will find the actions of your opponents to be revealing. With each additional bit of information, you are piecing together the storyline and doing your best to predict the ending. Let's look at two different examples of a poker player attempting a bluff. In the first example, a tight opponent raises pre-flop from early position (any position where a player can act before most of the other players), so we are likely to give him credit for a strong hand (since it takes a strong hand to raise from early position with so many players yet to act behind you). If he continues to bet aggressively throughout the hand, it is unlikely that anyone will call him unless they also have a strong hand.

Conversely, suppose our opponent raises pre-flop but then just checks after the flop. We check behind him. Now, to make things more complicated, suppose that after the turn, our opponent bets again. Is he betting because he has a strong hand or because he thinks our hand is weak? This second scenario is more confusing to us, which naturally leads to skepticism. When players are skeptical, they are much more likely to call. If you are going to bluff in poker, your opponents have to believe you. They are more likely to believe you if you tell a consistent story. You tell a consistent story by betting with strength throughout. If you waffle in your betting, you are sending mixed messages. When you send mixed messages, you greatly enhance your chances of meeting resistance.

Think about the message you want to send when you are negotiating. You want to be consistent in your approach and in your arguments. If you deviate at all from the rationale behind your argument, you are going to create confusion. Say you represent a Big League Conglomerate that manufactures a whole variety of clothing and accessories. All Star Jeans is going out of business, and the All Star trademark is up for sale. Big League wants to buy the trademark. During the negotiations, you want to know if the All Star mark is valid only for jeans or if they have rights for other goods. Even though you state that you want the trademark only for jeans, you want to know that the mark won't be diluted by someone else putting out cheap T-shirts with the All Star mark. A heated discussion follows, and there is a real question as to what rights, if any, the seller has in the trademark outside of blue jeans. As the argument intensifies, you state that you may want to use the trademark for pocketbooks and you really need to know how strong this trademark is across different product categories.

Now, you have told an inconsistent story. You started out stating your case in the defensive. That is, you didn't want someone diluting the trademark, even though your sole intention was to use it for jeans. Then, you let it be known that you may have intentions of using this trademark for other goods. The seller is naturally going to be skeptical of your intentions. She's going to be wondering if you are going to use the trademark for pocketbooks, what else do you envision using it for? You have now planted a seed in her mind that this trademark may have more value to you.

PLAY HARD

To be a winning poker player requires discipline and consistent execution. One mistake can be very costly. Every move a successful poker player makes is to maximize her profit or minimize her loss. The money you do not lose is as important as the money you win. Not winning the most money you can with a winning hand is as big a mistake as losing money with a hand that you should not have played in the first place.

Poker is a subtle, complex game with infinite possibilities. A good player relies on, among other things, experience, math, observation, and instinct to finesse her way through a poker game. One modest-sized pot an hour can be the difference between winning and losing over the long run. In order to win that one extra pot per hour requires a player to be on top of her game all of the time. She must combine a consistent effort with an unflinching concentration. She must never relax or let down her guard. She must do everything in her power to maximize her overall profit.

Even then, there will be plenty of sessions when a good poker player loses money. Some things just cannot be controlled no matter how hard one tries. Luck plays a big part in poker. While luck tends to even out in the long run and the better players will eventually succeed, luck in the short term can wreak havoc on even the best player's bankroll. The ability of a player to stay in and continue with a strong effort in the face of adversity will go a long way in determining her ultimate success.

The complexities we face in negotiations can be as myriad as those faced at the poker table. Fortunately, the lessons learned from poker can prove invaluable in facing the dilemmas of negotiating. We cannot always control every factor, but if we put forth a consistent and steady effort in all aspects of our negotiations, we can ensure success in most cases and in the long run.

It's hard not to have letdowns in poker. Over the course of a long session, it can be difficult to maintain both your focus and your ambition. I know when I am way ahead during a poker session, I may take a hand off or not extract every bet I can from a winning hand. That's just not good enough. One mistake can be costly in poker.

Similarly, you cannot afford a letdown in negotiations. If you are winning a lot of points, don't let down your guard. Don't dismiss an issue or let your opponent win one when you don't have to and when it matters to you. I'm not discussing compromises that are often critical to a successful negotiation. I'm talking about letting down your guard or resting on your laurels or losing focus or whatever else may affect your ability to negotiate hard. Poker requires a killer instinct. Good players don't let up on their opponents when they are down. The same thing holds true in negotiating. When you have leverage, you must implement it to maximum value. If you don't have leverage, you must fight to get it. Do your research ahead of time so you are as informed as possible. If things are slipping away at the negotiating table, take a break. One of the biggest mistakes poker players make is not taking a break or even calling it a day when they are playing poorly and can no longer stay focused.

There are no rules written in stone for negotiations. There is nothing that says you can't end a session early and start again the next day. Even if this isn't practicable, you can always at least take a break to get up to speed so you can negotiate at your best.

SEMI-BLUFF IF YOU HAVE OUTS

Everyone knows what a bluff is in poker. However, semi-bluffs are a more integral and implemented tool of the experienced player. A poker player bluffs when he knows he is beat but feels that his opponent is vulnerable. He bets hoping that his opponent will believe he has a strong hand and fold. In fact, the bluffer's only hope is that his opponent folds. If his opponent calls, he loses. A semi-bluff is different. In a semi-bluff situation, the player making the semi-bluff is behind with more cards to come. There are a number of cards that could make a winning hand for the semi-bluffer (these cards are called outs for the semi-bluffer). For instance, Player S may have a pair of threes with a single ace and four to a spade flush (i.e., one more spade will give him a flush). His opponent has a pair of jacks and is ahead of Player S at the moment. Player S semi-bluffs here, hoping his opponent folds his hand and concedes the pot. However, if the opponent calls the bet, all is not lost. Player S has a lot of outs. A three, an ace, or any spade will give Player S a winning hand.

In your everyday life, negotiate from strength when you have outs. Outs allow you to play your hand more aggressively than you otherwise would. If you have three qualified contractors coming in at approximately the same price to finish your basement, then use that to your advantage. Negotiate for a better deal. Ask Contractor A for a better price (or extra lighting), saying you are willing to sign a contract if the concession is made. If Contractor A refuses, move on to Contractor B or C. Even if you prefer Contractor A, you can always go back to him at the original price.

If you have a good, secure job but are looking for a new and better job, do not settle. Take advantage of your current job security. Only be willing to switch if the new position is a significant improvement. Changing jobs is a big move and not something you can do that often. Employers value loyalty. You do not want to change jobs for trivial reasons. Be selective. You have outs—your present job is secure. Negotiate with your new employer from strength. Let him know that you are happy with your current job and you are willing to leave only for the ideal situation. Negotiate for that ideal situation, including pay and benefits. You have outs. If you do not get what you want this time, there will be more opportunities down the road. Of course, if your present job is not secure, your negotiating becomes more tenuous. You don't need to volunteer that information, but you don't want to be misleading. How shaky your current situation is will dictate how strong a negotiating stance you will take. In these situations, don't be afraid to negotiate for what you want, just don't back yourself in a corner. Never phrase something as a deal breaker. Instead, take a soft approach and state that this is what you were hoping for, which is consistent with market value. If your number can't be met, you may need a few days to consider the original proposal.

Protecting your hand is always critical. If you're looking for a job, don't share this information with any of your co-workers. Even if you trust someone, they may confide in someone else, believing it won't go further.

LET YOUR OPPONENT DO YOUR BIDDING FOR YOU

The key to success in poker is playing every hand to maximum value. When you have a strong hand, it is not enough to win the pot. You want to win the most money you can with that hand. A common strategy of successful players is to let their opponent do their bidding for them. For instance, if a player (let's call him Player S for "sensible") has a strong hand and he is up against an aggressive player (Player X). Player S has position on Player X, so Player S may allow Player X to control the betting in order to extract the maximum number of chips out of Player X. If Player X acts first and is the type of player to bet out until stopped, why stop him? Player S would be smart to just call Player X until the last round of betting. On the last round of betting, Player S would raise and Player X might call, since he already has so much money invested in the pot. However, if Player S raised Player X in an earlier round, there is a greater likelihood that Player X would fold, realizing that he was probably beat. Player X is the type of player who will bet as long as he is the aggressor. Once someone pushes back, however, he is likely to fold if he does not have a strong hand. A good player uses that to his advantage. When the good player has a strong hand, he would be smart to let Player X do his betting for him.

Everyone knows a Player X type in real life. This is the person who does not want to take no for an answer. This is the person who will keep pushing until you push back. Depending on the situation, use that to your advantage. If a business associate approaches you with a proposition that he is insistent upon, then let him do the bidding for you. Remain noncommittal and see how far he will compromise. Let him make concessions on his own. Let him negotiate against himself. Once he gets to a point at which you are comfortable, fire back. Negotiate from there.

Many car salesmen are notorious Player X types. They do not want you leaving the dealership without purchasing a car. They do not want to take no for an answer. They enjoy success, though, because most customers do not know how to deal with them. Most customers want to leave with a car. Thus, they either fight back right away or get pressured into making a deal.

Try letting the salesman do the bidding. Ask him for his best offer and then feign disinterest. Let him know you still have other dealerships to check out and other brands to look into. If you have done your research, you will know what constitutes a fair price. So, start walking to induce him to come down. Not every salesman will come down, but you will be surprised by how many do. Circle the lot, checking out other cars in a nonchalant manner. Wait it out. Let the salesman get close to your figure and then fire back. Work the situation for maximum value. Let him bet all the way to the river before you raise him. At that point, he is not likely to fold, since he has invested too much time. He is likely to see your raise and pay you off.

DO NOT CONFUSE LOUTISH ACTING OUT WITH COLORFUL BEHAVIOR

There is no question that the recent explosion in poker's popularity is directly linked to the ever-expanding television coverage of tournament poker. While the television coverage has certainly been great for poker overall, it is not without its drawbacks. One of the biggest drawbacks has been the increase in loutish, and even downright obnoxious, behavior at the poker table. With television cameras hovering around, some players feel the need to draw attention to themselves. At the 2006 main event of the World Series of Poker, there were over eighty-five hundred entrants. While the majority of those entrants were competing for the $12,000,000 first-place prize, others were competing for face time in front of the cameras. Colorful characters, of which there are many in poker, make for great television. Unfortunately, there are some who confuse loutish actions with colorful behavior. They talk trash, stalk around the tables, disparage their opponents' play, scream up and down when they get lucky, and make other less obvious gestures that are outside of accepted poker etiquette. Since so many new players are being introduced to the game from television, it should be no surprise that there has been a great increase in loutish behavior in card rooms over the last few years. What these louts do not realize is that not only is this bad etiquette, it ultimately hurts their game. You want to control your opponents; you do not want to antagonize them. Your want your opponents to respect and fear you. You do not want your opponents gunning for you.

Be firm in your everyday negotiations. Be strong and decisive. Control every aspect of the negotiations. However, remember to always be civil, polite, and respectful of your adversaries. Ultimately, your goal is to get the most favorable deal you can. You seriously undermine your ability to accomplish that goal if you antagonize the other side. It is human nature to fight back when attacked. Think how you would react if someone acted obnoxiously toward you. You would not stand for it and you should not expect anyone else to, either. If you engage in loutish behavior during negotiations, one of two things can happen. First, the other side may really dig in their heels and fight back on every issue—even those they do not care about. They may take unreasonable positions and be far less likely to compromise, since the negotiations have taken on a personal tone. Or, alternatively, they may just walk away. Life is too short to waste time with louts. Why negotiate with a rude and obnoxious person when there are always other potential deals out there?

TAKE WHAT YOU WANT, NOT JUST WHAT YOUR OPPONENT GIVES YOU

There is a common cliché in sports that "you should take what your opponent gives you." That advice is as sound as it is obvious. My main problem with it, however, is that it does not go far enough. Sure, you should take what your opponent gives you. But you should also take what you want. This is especially true in poker. There will be plenty of poker games in which none of the players has a particularly strong hand. It then becomes a test of wills as to who will win the pot. There will be plenty of hands when one opponent is willing to concede the pot. There will also be plenty when nobody is willing to give up the pot.

If you have ever watched television coverage of a final table of a major poker tournament, you will know what I am talking about. Often these hands end up being played heads-up when there are big pots and a lot at stake. Neither player is willing to concede anything. These players who are among the top in the world will battle for that pot. Each wants to take all of those chips in the center for himself. It then becomes a battle of who can outwit, outplay, and out-will the others. Who wants to take that pot the most?

Let me offer a real-life example of the benefits of taking what you want and not just what your opponent offers you. Say you are putting a bid in on a house and you would love to get the house for $225,000, although you would be willing to go as high as $237,000. Unbeknownst to you, the seller would love to get $240,000 for the house but is willing to sell for $230,000. If you go into the negotiations with the attitude that you will take what the seller will give you, you are guaranteed to end up paying somewhere between $230,000 and $237,000; most likely you will be a lot closer to $237,000 than $230,000. Why is that? Because you are only willing to take what the seller is willing to concede. At this point, there is no reason to believe that the seller is willing to concede anything at all, and he may hold out until he gets you to your maximum number.

Now, if you go in with the attitude that you are going to take what you want, your chances for a lower price rise dramatically. State your case why the house is worth $225,000. Make it clear that $225,000 is a fair price and represents a true market value. Most important, make it clear that $225,000—and not a dime more—is what you are willing to pay. Outwit, outthink, and outplay your opponent. Remember to use all of your negotiating and poker skills in your discussions. At the forefront of all those negotiations should be a red light reminder that you are there to take what you want. Do all that, and you are much more likely to get that price closer to $230,000 and maybe even lower. If there are many others bidding on the house, then it may make sense to look for alternatives where you can be assured of getting your price.

MAINTAIN A GOOD POKER FACE

Even if you have never played poker, you have certainly heard of the importance of maintaining a good poker face. Having a good poker face is more than just maintaining a stoic expression. It is having complete control of your actions and mannerisms in order to prevent your opponent from getting a read on you. That is just one aspect, though, of maintaining a poker face. You want to have control of your entire body. You do not want to play with your chips a certain way when you have a strong hand. You do not want to take a second peek at your cards to make sure you really do have those aces. Most important, you do not want your betting patterns to be a dead giveaway of your hand.

What's the best way to ensure you maintain a poker face? To gain as much experience as possible. Since the potential situations in poker are limitless, the more experience one has, the quicker one can react. When you react quickly, you maintain control of your body language and actions and avoid giving tells. It is extremely hard to ponder the situation for any length of time without giving away a clue to your intentions.

When I was a young associate working with a large law firm in

New York, I would frequently sit in and assist on major negotiations. As was the custom, it would be a few years before I was leading negotiations. However, due to extenuating circumstances, I found myself leading the negotiations on behalf of the buyer in a substantial acquisition of a business. The partner in charge was working on two negotiations simultaneously and was literally running back and forth between two conference rooms. Finally, he chose to concentrate on the other transaction and left me in charge to finish up negotiating a definite acquisition agreement. I was both excited and nervous for the opportunity. My primary goal was to not screw up anything. We were almost done with the negotiations and only had a few sections left to finish. The attorney for the seller was a senior partner at a well-respected Boston law firm (let's call him Mr. Senior), and the two of us sat down to complete the negotiations. I was visibly nervous, and to my adversary's credit, he gave me plenty of time to mull over every point. When we got to the section on environmental liability, Mr. Senior handed me a rather lengthy provision drafted by his partner who specializes in environmental law. Now, environmental law is a rather specialized area of law and one I did not have much experience in. I read the provision carefully. On the first read, I must have done a double take, because the provision seemed to benefit the buyer (my client) rather than the seller. I reread the provision two more times to make sure. As I said, my primary goal was to not screw anything up. Finally, convinced that the provision really was in our favor, I said the change was acceptable. Well, my body language certainly gave something away, because Mr. Senior quickly grabbed the sheet back and read it for himself. He crossed out the provision and said that they dropped the point. So much for my poker face.

Of course, the good news was that Mr. Senior's actions certainly validated my interpretation of the provision. The bad news is that I had cost my client a point by my inexperience and subsequent tentativeness. If I had been more experienced, I would have read the provision once and said something like, "I can live with this, what's next?"

While I accomplished my goal of not screwing up, I was not the best advocate that I could have been for my client. Before entering any negotiation, learn as much as you can about the subject at hand so you can maintain a good poker face.

OBSERVE YOUR OPPONENT'S BEHAVIOR

It should go without saying that observing your opponent's behavior is extremely important to your ultimate success at the poker table. Five years ago, this chapter would not have been as necessary. However, we are now living in a virtual world. Online poker has exploded in the last few years. There are many benefits to playing online. One can gain a lot of experience quickly by playing in the comfort of one's own home. You can face every situation you would in a brick and mortar card room. The one thing you cannot duplicate, however, is the face-to-face contact. Sure, you can chat online. You can even pick up on the betting patterns of your online opponents. You cannot pick up on your opponents' body language, though.

Many studies claim that nonverbal communication makes up over 50 percent of our overall communication. Even if that figure is high, there is no doubt that body language counts for a lot, and there is only one way to ensure that you are getting the entire picture. You must meet face to face.

Modern technology has made for quick and easy communication. Fax machines, cell phones, e-mail, and instant messaging allow us to maintain constant contact with just about anyone anywhere in the world. The need to meet in person has been diminished greatly. Most communication can be accomplished efficiently and cheaply without having to leave our home or office. There is even video conferencing, which allows us to see each other. In many cases, the cost in time and money is not worth traveling to have a face-to-face meeting.

In many cases, however, it is well worth making the effort to meet in person. Do not let the conveniences of modern technology keep you from getting the complete picture. Although you can gain invaluable experience playing online poker, there is no substitute for playing in a live poker game. That is the only way one can truly learn to become a better player. If you have a negotiation or meeting of importance, give it the attention and respect it deserves. Meet in person if at all possible.

ALL PARTIES NEED TO BELIEVE THEY HAVE DONE WELL

When playing poker, you do not want to antagonize your opponents. Most recreational players come to the table to enjoy themselves. They view it as entertainment, and any money they lose is part of their entertainment budget. They are there to enjoy themselves, and the money that they may win or lose is secondary. So let them enjoy themselves. Encourage their play. If they make a dumb decision and draw out on you, compliment them on the nice hand. As noted earlier, if they keep making those kinds of plays, eventually you will win their money. When they lose a hand, let them know that they are playing well but they are just experiencing some bad luck right now. Eventually, that luck will turn around their way. As simple as these concepts sound, it is amazing how many otherwise good players cannot control themselves. As we've seen, they berate lesser players for poor decisions. They create such an unfriendly atmosphere that these lesser players who just want to have a good time get up and leave and either go to another table or they go play a different game entirely, such as blackjack. The bottom line is that the lesser player is taking his easy money someplace else and the otherwise good player has just made his own job of winning more difficult.

Negotiations are always much easier if you can make everyone feel that they are doing well. Less-experienced attorneys and businesspeople often feel the need to impress everyone with their knowledge rather than trying to reach the desired result. I remember one instance where I was negotiating an acquisition agreement and I had a younger attorney (let's call him Junior, Esq.) assisting me. We were representing the buyer and we had inserted a paragraph that allowed us to contact the seller's vendors without liability prior to the closing. (The buyer in this case may want to contact these vendors as part of his due diligence investigation. The seller may agree but will want to be indemnified if the deal falls through and the buyer says something to harm the reputation of the seller.) The seller's attorney (let's call him Seller, Esq.) strongly objected to this provision, calling it highly unusual and unacceptable. Before I could respond, Junior, Esq. went off on Seller, Esq. Junior, Esq. insisted that this was a perfectly standard clause and no way were we going to change it. Of course, this only antagonized the Seller, Esq. further. I finally calmed them both down. I then explained to Seller, Esq. that he made an excellent point, but that what he did not know was that in this particular case the seller had asked our client (the buyer) to contact some of the seller's vendors to inform them of the deal and let them know that if the deal was consummated, they would get paid. Since we were doing this at the seller's request, we certainly did not want to have liability. If we did not have this provision in the contract, I would be forced to advise my client not to contact the vendors and the entire deal would be in jeopardy. Seller, Esq. confirmed this with the seller and conceded the point. Now at this point, we should have just moved on to the next issue. Yet, Junior, Esq. would not let it go. He still insisted on trying to prove his point that this was a standard clause and that Seller, Esq. was dead wrong. What was the point of doing this? We had already won the point. All it accomplished was to get Seller, Esq. worked up again and make the remaining negotiations more difficult. If Junior, Esq. had just followed my lead, Seller, Esq. would have felt good about his position even though he lost the point to extenuating circumstances, and we could have moved on in a better negotiating position.

UNDERSTAND AND EVALUATE ALL OF YOUR OPTIONS

Before making any decision in poker, you must evaluate and understand all of your options. Any time its your turn to act, you have the option of checking, betting, raising, or calling, depending on the situation. Each of these options has consequences. In order to pick the optimal move, you need to understand what each of those consequences may be and the likelihood of those consequences happening. The idea of poker is to maximize your profit. In order to do that, you must play in a way to get the desired consequence that you are seeking. For example, in no-limit Hold 'em, your options are even greater because you may bet any amount up to all of the chips on your table. Now, let's say you find yourself in a hand with what you know to be the absolute best hand. You are guaranteed to win the hand, so now your focus changes to how you can best maximize your profit. Ideally, you would bet your entire chip stack and have all of your opponents call, giving you the greatest possible outcome. The likelihood of your opponents calling such a big bet, however, may be slim. If there is not a lot of money in the pot or if your opponents are unlikely to have strong hands, then it is doubtful that they will call a big bet. You would then probably want to bet something less than the maximum. You would want to find that amount that your opponent is likely to call or, if you are lucky, even raise. You may even consider checking, in the hope that your opponent will sense weakness and then bet out himself. On the other hand, if your opponent has a strong but losing hand and there is already a lot of money in the pot, you may want to bet the maximum, since it is likely he will call. The point is, you want to consider all of your options to find the one that will maximize your profit or minimize your loss, depending on the circumstances.

In any negotiation, your ultimate goal is to get the best deal and extract the most concessions you can from the other side. In a perfect world (for you), you would demand every point you wanted and your adversary would concede. Of course, that is not the world that we live in. Thus, you must consider all of your options and pick a course of action that will offer you the most favorable transaction. Prioritize those issues that are important to you and then develop a strategy for achieving them. Do not demand too much on lesser issues if by doing so you cause the other side to fold or walk away or dig their heels in deeper on an issue that is more important to you.

Whenever you have leverage, use it, but be careful not to overplay your hand. Strong hands are wonderful to hold, but if you overplay them, you will cause your opponent to walk away and you will have nothing to show for that great hand.

UNDERSTAND AND EVALUATE YOUR OPPONENTS' OPTIONS

In order to properly understand and evaluate your own options, you must understand and evaluate your opponents' options. Poker, like everything else in life, is not played in a vacuum. So many times I watch beginning players get a strong hand early on and bet it for all it's worth, only to see all of their opponents fold. If the novice had just taken the time to understand and evaluate his opponents' options, he could have greatly increased his profit. By exercising a little patience, the novice could have waited for his opponents to catch a hand or make a play for the pot. The further along and more involved a player is in a hand, the harder it is for him to fold. It is much easier for a player to fold early in a hand when he has not committed much to the pot.

In any negotiation, know your adversary's options. If you are buying a house in a resale, know what options the seller has. Are there other potential buyers? Is their seller in a hurry to sell? If the house has been on the market for a while and you are the only potential buyer and the seller has already moved out, then you should be able to make any reasonable offer. In addition, you should be able to take a hard line after the home inspection. Now that the seller has accepted your offer, he will want to salvage the deal. He does not want to lose the only buyer that will sign a contract. Furthermore, depending on the nature of the problems revealed by the inspection, the seller may have to disclose those problems to any other potential buyers. The seller is now very involved in the hand. He is pot committed at this point.

The further along you are in any deal, the harder it will be for either party to walk away. People do not want to have to start over again. Recognizing this should help you use it to your advantage. Just be careful not to overplay your hand, because you also have a lot invested at this point and you do not want to walk away empty-handed for your efforts.

SOMETIMES NOTHING MAKES A PRETTY GOOD HAND

If you are going to be proactive and not wait for the perfect hand to come your way, then sometimes you will play a less than desirable hand. You'll seize the moment when you see an opportunity to exploit. If you sense weakness on your opponents' parts, then it will make sense at times to implement a bluff. If you are going to be a successful poker player, then you're going to have to win more hands than just those when you're dealt the best cards. If everyone won the hands when they had the best cards, then things would pretty much even out. Not to mention that you would be stuck in a pretty boring game.

There will be times when it is ideal to bluff. Those times come when you know your opponent has you beat but you also think that your opponent's hand isn't particularly strong, so he is likely to fold if you make a strong bet. In these situations, your hand is irrelevant. You are reading your opponent. Perhaps he has a tell or a pattern of playing that gives his hand away. As long as you do not project weakness and you take the initiative in betting at the pot first, you stand a great chance of bluffing your opponent out of the pot. It does not matter if you have nothing because you are not planning on getting called.

Now, you certainly cannot go around bluffing your way through life. Life does not work that way. What you can do, however, is remember how important it is to read your opponent. Whenever you are in a negotiation, do not allow yourself to get so consumed with your own vulnerabilities that you ignore the Achilles' heel of the other side. For instance, if you have been looking forever for that dream house and you think you finally have found it, do not put undue pressure on yourself. Perhaps the seller has his own pressure because he's already put down a deposit on another house. Always take the time to understand the other side's position in order to provide you with some balance to the negotiation.

CHANNELING ANGER

I generally believe that anger is a wasted emotion and can be destructive at both the poker and negotiating table. A clear head that can remain objective and rational will win the day. Over the years, I have learned to be thick-skinned and not let things get to me. Obnoxious players and negotiators are to be sized up and bested with an appropriate strategy. A lucky player is to be congratulated with the comfort of your knowing that he will soon give away his chips. Every once in a while, though, I'll cross paths with a player who is as fortunate as he is rude and I won't be able to contain myself. I rarely lose my temper or make disparaging comments. In fact, I can think of only one time in recent memory that I snapped off a remark.

I was playing a single-table tournament in which the top three places paid, although first place was to receive the bulk of the money. One player was winning in spite of his every effort to give away his chips. Time and time again, he would catch a miracle card to beat an opponent. He was making horrible decisions but was being bailed out by the poker gods. Of course, he didn't see it that way. He thought he was playing well and made sure to express that to everyone else. By the time we got down to four players, he had a monster chip lead. He had more chips than the rest of us combined. I knew it was only a matter of time before he imploded and lost, but even so, he would be tough to beat, since he had so many chips.

At one point, he had close to $40,000 in chips while I had around $1,000. With such a short stack, I had to take a chance with my first playable hand. I moved all-in with a pair of eights, and my adversary called with ace-nine. He hit an ace on the flop, but the river brought an eight and I survived. To my astonishment, my opponent went off on a tirade about how lucky I was. Never mind that I was a favorite when all the money went in before the flop. Normally, I would just nod my head in agreement, but this time, I couldn't control myself. I had a couple of choice words for him and his close friendship with fortune.

That release was therapeutic. My awareness and focus increased exponentially. Rather than remain angry, I channeled all of that energy into beating this guy. Sure, I was way behind in chips, but I was way ahead in skill. I managed to slowly build my stack up and then eliminated the other players. By the time I got heads-up with my obnoxious foe, he had only a slight chip lead. He offered to split the remaining prize money evenly, but I was in no mood to deal. I politely declined and then I completely annihilated him and took the first-place prize money.

Losing one's cool at the negotiating table is rarely, if ever, effective. Obnoxious negotiators are a lot like obnoxious poker players. You adjust to their style and let them make mistakes. Screamers have no credibility. Ironically, a well-timed burst of anger, however, can be a very powerful strategy against a screamer. If there is an audience of people with a vested interest in the negotiations at hand, you can be sure that just about everyone will be tiring of the loudmouth's act. Even those on his side will be embarrassed by his shenanigans. Instead of getting loud and stooping to his level, channel that anger into something effective. Wait for a critical point in the negotiations and let it be known that you are sick of his act, stating your point in a deliberate and articulate manner that is wrapped in a hushed tone of anger: that is sure to get everyone's attention.

THE POKER EXPERIENCE

A Failure to Communicate

I played in private games for well over ten years before I made my first venture into a casino to play. I visited the Trump Taj Mahal poker room with some friends. It was the biggest room at the time and to this day remains one of the best places to play in Atlantic City. I would become a more frequent visitor in the later '90s, continuing to this present day, playing in everything from cash games to big tournaments there. On my first visit, though, I was just another tourist who believed he could rule the poker table due to past success with friends and colleagues.

I sat down at the cheapest table available, which was $1 to $3 spread-limit seven-card stud. What that means is that you can bet or raise anywhere from $1 to $3 dollars in any betting round. There was a maximum of three raises per round. Even at these limits, if enough players stayed in the betting (which was often the case), the pots could grow significantly for a player's initial entry into casino poker. Sitting down with a table full of strangers, I was definitely a little nervous. I wanted to make sure that I knew all of the rules and proper etiquette. I didn't want to make a mistake, as I did at our church carnival years before. I had played a lot of seven-card stud in the past, so I was fairly confident in my ability to at least hold my own. For the first hour, I was essentially holding my own when disaster struck, due solely to my own ignorance and self-consciousness.

I got involved in a hand where I started with a pair of aces—a very strong starting hand in seven-card stud. There was a lot of action in this hand with quite a few players staying in. My aces had not improved by the sixth card, and with so many players still in the pot, I wasn't sure I was going to win unless I received the third ace with my last card. Even though I hadn't seen another ace, the odds were still not good. At the time, my hand looked like this (ace-two)-ace-ten-three-four (the cards in parentheses being my down cards). Whenever

I had played seven-card stud in private games, we always declared ahead of time whether an ace could be high or low. If you look at my cards, you can see where that could make a big difference in my hand. If my last card was a five, I would have a straight (ace-two-three-four-five) if an ace counted as low (as a one). Of course, I now know that an ace can always be used as high or low in any civilized seven-card stud game. At the time, though, my frame of reference had me in doubt. Sure enough, the last card I received was a five. Now, I had a real dilemma. I knew that my pair of aces would not win the hand, however, I was fairly sure that a straight would.

In every game I had played prior to this experience, you had to declare your hand. In another words, if I turned over my cards and said I had a pair of aces, then I would be bound by that, even if I did have a straight. The last thing I wanted to do, however, was announce a straight and then find out that I didn't have one because an ace could not be counted as a low card. The second-to-last thing I wanted to do was ask if an ace could be used as a low card and effectively announce my hand to the table. When the action got to me, I tried to ask the player next to me in a whisper if an ace could be used as a low card. This player was slightly inebriated, and I wasn't sure if he quite understood my question. More significantly, I wasn't sure if I could trust his answer. So, I folded. The minute I did, a lightbulb seemed to go off in the drunken state of the other player's mind, and he picked up my cards to look at what I had. He then chastised me for throwing away a straight. As it turned out, I threw away the winning hand and cost myself a rather sizable pot.

To make matters worse, I found out later that night that in casino poker the cards speak for themselves. That is, you don't have to declare your hand. All you have to do is turn over your cards and it's up to the dealer to decide who wins. Even if you declare the wrong hand, your strongest hand still counts. If I had declared a pair of aces, I still would have won if you assume that the dealer would recognize my straight. I would still caution that you are better off stating your hand or at least knowing its true value when you turn it over so there is no mistake.

As much as I thought I knew what I was doing, I still tripped myself up by not possessing as much knowledge as I should have had before commencing play. Poker is hard enough without putting myself at a disadvantage from the start with my ignorance. What was really disturbing in retrospect was my self-consciousness. There's an old adage that goes something like this: "It is better to remain silent and be thought a fool than to speak up and remove all doubt."

That's great advice for fools, but for the rest of us, it's horrible advice. It's much better to speak up and be informed than to remain silent and in ignorance. Whether I'm seeking information or making a point, I'm not going to be gun-shy. Sure, I may not always make the greatest point, but if I don't speak up, I'll be thought the fool. I'd much rather take my chances expressing my opinion.

6. ALL-IN: CLIMB THE CORPORATE LADDER AND WIN

Before I sit down to a poker table, I undergo a total transformation of character. I leave behind my everyday self and take on a new persona. In poker, it's destroy or be destroyed. No matter how friendly their demeanor, those nine other people at the table are trying to take my money. I have to be my most ruthless and cunning self to succeed in this environment. Short of cheating (which is never acceptable), there are no ethical guidelines. In fact, deception is not only accepted, it is expected. Deception is a critical part of the game.

As poker has gained in popularity and become part of mainstream American culture, we have come to admire the skills associated with a successful poker player. No one likes to view himself as a sucker. Each of us wants to believe that he has a good poker face and can outwit others when the chips are down. Certainly, the skills necessary for poker can be used effectively in the corporate world. As we begin this chapter, however, it's important to recognize one critical difference between the workplace and the poker room.

Corporations large and small spend substantial dollars on such things as increasing morale, building team spirit, and instilling values along with a company mission statement. They do this because it's important to remember that your co-workers are your teammates, not your enemies. As an employee, you are working for the common good of the company good, not your individual good.

At first blush, then, it would seem that many of the principles learned in the poker room would be at odds with those in the workplace. I would disagree with that assumption. Still, I do think that it is extremely important to keep these principles in context when applying them to the corporate environment. Yes, there is competition in climbing the corporate ladder. However, unlike the poker room, there are strict ethical guidelines that should never be crossed. Deception should never be practiced nor tolerated when working with your fellow employees. With that in mind, let's take a look at how you can use poker principles to further your career.

PLAN FOR A LIFETIME OF SUCCESS

Poker players don't worry about short-term gains and losses as much as they play each and every hand one step at a time. The winning player looks at poker as one lifelong game that she intends to win. There will be good days and bad days and ups and downs along the way, but she will hang in there, looking for ways to improve in order to make as many correct decisions as possible.

Careers are typically measured over decades, not years. Even when you hear about so-called overnight success stories, the person enjoying that success has usually paid his dues. People become successful by trusting their talent and skill to rise to the top over the long term. They do not look for shortcuts that bring them short-term success but leave them well short of achieving their long-term goals. If you want to be an actor, you do not start out by going to auditions. Even if you were lucky enough to book a job, your performance would probably keep you from achieving long-term success. Rather, the aspiring actor would first take lessons and hone his craft before trying to get work. No matter what the profession, if you have the necessary skills and apply yourself, you will eventually rise to the top. Cream always does.

FIND YOUR NICHE

A common mistake of beginning Hold 'em players is to play hands that are easily dominated. What do I mean by dominated? Let's look at a specific example. A favorite practice for the neophyte poker player is to play any ace coupled with another card. While a starting hand like ace-king is an extremely strong one, a hand like ace-nine can spell a lot of trouble. The reason is that the ace-nine hand is dominated by any other hand holding an ace with a second card of a rank higher than a nine. Since hands like ace-ten, ace-jack, ace-queen, and ace-king are good to great starting hands, depending on the situation, you are more likely to be up against an opponent with one of these hands than you are an opponent holding a hand you would have dominated, such as nine-six.

Let's say you decide to play ace-nine and three other players decide to pay to see a flop as well. The flop comes ace-seven-two. This has the appearance of being a very good flop for you. Yet, it spells trouble. With three other players in the pot, there is a fairly good chance that one of your opponents has an ace with a bigger kicker than you have. If that's the case, you could lose a lot of money on this hand, since you will have a hard time folding. But what if no one else has an ace? What if you have the best hand here? That's great and it's certainly better than being up against an ace with a bigger kicker. Yet, you are unlikely to win much money. Your opponents will be very concerned that someone else will have an ace and they are unlikely to commit any more money to the pot.

As a poker player, if I'm in a hand with a number of other opponents, I'd much rather have a hand like four-five than ace-nine. With the four-five, there is a much greater probability that I have what are referred to as *live cards*. That is, my opponents are unlikely to be holding hands that contain a four or a five. Thus, those cards are live for me. If a four or five appear on the board, those cards will help me and no one else. With a flop like ten-four-five, I am likely to have the best hand. Additionally, say I have two opponents playing ace-jack and ace-ten, respectively. There are only two aces remaining in the deck that can help them. Any time my opponents share common cards, that increases my chances for success.

With my four-five, I will also have a much deeper understanding of where I stand compared to the others. I have picked a niche for myself that will either succeed or not. When I play that ace-nine, I will have a hard time folding when I flop an ace, even if I suspect my opponent has me beat with a hand such as ace-jack. With four-five, I can easily fold my hand unless I get a very favorable flop. If the flop is king-nine-five, I know I do not have a strong hand, even with my pair of fives.

So, how does all of this relate to the workplace? The short answer is that if everyone is playing aces, try some other cards. For the longer answer, let's explore this in more detail. The obvious solution is not always the optimal solution. If a number of your colleagues are playing the ace-high hand, then there is a good chance that your company's competitors are as well. For instance, say you are in the marketing department of Widget Company, and your colleagues in the department all come from traditional media backgrounds. They each advocate print and television advertising for your company. On the other hand, you are a big proponent of attempting things outside of the ordinary and have some great ideas for so-called viral marketing campaigns that do not cost much money but can have a huge impact if they work. (Viral marketing campaigns rely on word of mouth and often use new medium such as free video downloads.) That's a four-five hand. It is not as obvious, but if it works, it will do extremely well.

Now let's look at this situation from your employer's point of view. All other things being equal, there are four strong employees of which only one can rise. Three of those employees are adept at playing aces, yet only one is strong at playing four-five. If you are among one of those three playing aces, you'd better be the one playing ace-king. Otherwise, you have the weaker ace than your counterpart. Each of those marketers advocating the traditional media route has the pressure of coming out with the best ad campaign. You don't have to have the best viral marketing campaign, you just have to have a successful one.

SURVIVAL VERSUS CHIP ACCUMULATION

The strategies in tournament poker are quite different from those used in more traditional cash games. In tournaments, each player starts with the same number of chips. Play continues until one player has all of the chips. Payouts are determined based on when each player is eliminated. Typically, the top 10 percent of players will be in the money or make a return on their investment. However, the payouts are weighted heavily toward the top. For example, say one hundred players enter a poker tournament and pay a $100 entry fee. The tenth-place finisher may win a little over $100. He will get his entry fee back and maybe an extra $25. The first-place finisher will win in the neighborhood of $3,500. That's a big difference. Notice that players finishing between eleventh and one-hundredth receive nothing. Since results in poker are judged by how much money is made, the player finishing in eleventh place has fared no better than the player finishing in one-hundredth. One could even argue that he has fared worse, since he has invested substantially more time and has suffered costs in other opportunities.

To understand tournaments better, let's look at some of the fundamental differences between tournament play and cash games. Chips used in tournaments have no value outside of the tournament. Players cannot take leave the table with those chips and cash them out. Thus, they have no value other than to advance a player as far as possible in the tournament. Next, once a player is out of chips in a tournament, he is eliminated. He cannot reach into his pocket and buy more chips. Finally, in order to move the action along in a tournament, the blinds are increased at predetermined time intervals. In a cash game, those levels are static. If you sit down to a cash game where the blinds are $5 to $10, it will stay at those levels all night. In a tournament, the blinds may increase every twenty minutes. So if you start out with blinds at $5 to $10, within a couple of hours, those blinds may be $200 to $400, which is quite a difference.

As you can imagine, tournament play creates some interesting dynamics. In a cash game, a player can wait all night for ideal opportunities. Whether he's up or down, he's free to leave the table at any time and cash out whatever chips he may have. If he runs out of chips, he can easily buy some more. Players in a tournament have to constantly strike a balance between holding onto their chips in order to avoid elimination while trying to gather as many chips as possible so they can advance far and win big money.

EXPLOIT ANY OPPORTUNITY WITH POSITIVE EXPECTED VALUE

Winning poker players are especially adept at exploiting for maximum profit any opportunity with a positive expected value. Even the slightest edge is worth playing. For instance, say you have pocket queens and you know your opponent has ace-king. Those pocket queens are a very slight favorite but a favorite nonetheless. They are approximately a 53 percent favorite. While this might not seem like much of an edge, when you are up against an equal opponent, you would be willing to push that edge to the maximum because you know by doing so, you give yourself the best chance to win in the long run.

There are a lot of opportunities out there that may not seem that significant, but if you consistently pursue them, you will do well in the long run. Work that extra hour, help out a co-worker with his project, and ask your boss what you can do to help. All of these have positive expected value in the long run. They may not pay immediate dividends, but if you do these things consistently then you will help your company and advance yourself.

DO NOT COUNT ON GETTING CARDS

If you play poker on a regular basis, you will get your fair share of good hands. So will everyone else. If you are relying on getting good cards to ensure your success, you might as well go play slots. As I've emphasized, there is a lot of luck in poker. But there is also a lot of skill. If poker were all luck, then in the long run everyone would end up with the money they started out with. Of course, that is not the case.

In poker, as in life, you must make your breaks. You must create opportunity where it appears that none exists. You cannot sit around all day waiting for something to fall in your lap. If you are willing to only play pocket aces, then you will not be playing very often. And when you do play, your opponents are sure to know what you have and will quickly fold to your bet, leaving you with little to show for your patience.

In poker, everything is situational. You must play the hand you are dealt. This does not mean that you should play every hand. Quite the contrary. You should only play when you perceive you have an advantage. There will be times when you have a weak hand but you sense your opponents do not have playable hands, either. This may be an opportune time to play. Conversely, there may be times when you have a rather strong hand but you sense one of your opponents has an extremely strong hand. While you have a very tempting hand to play, you should fold.

Unless you are one of the chosen ones who can walk through life and have everything handed to you, you cannot wait for that perfect hand to be dealt to you. Rather, you must always analyze your present situation in order to create opportunities for yourself. If there does not seem to be any chance for a promotion in your department at work, then create your own plan for expanding your responsibilities and present it to your boss. Gather as much information as you can about your possibilities. Ask your boss or human resources manager what you can do to advance. Inquire about potential opportunities in other departments. Be proactive. Do not wait for that dream position to be offered to you.

LEARN AND PLAY A FEW DIFFERENT GAMES

There are many different forms of poker. Games such as Hold 'em, Omaha, and seven-card stud are all very different. In addition, some games such as Omaha and seven-card stud can be played "hi-lo," meaning both the high hand and the low hand split the pot. Finally, the betting structure can completely change the nature of the game. Limit Hold 'em is a vastly different game from no-limit Hold 'em. The best players play most, if not all of the games. Even if a top player is better at one game, she will still try to play a number of different games. It is always beneficial to broaden your skill set. Since each game emphasizes different aspects of poker, by playing multiple games you become more well rounded. You gain different perspectives and sharpen skills that can only help your overall game. Additionally, players who are proficient in multiple games will never have trouble finding a table to their liking. Over time, games can come in and out of vogue. A well-rounded player will be able to change and thrive with the times.

No matter what your line of work, you can always benefit from learning a wide range of skills. Do not limit yourself. Take an interest in what your co-workers are doing. If you are working on a specific part of a project, take the time to understand the entire project. This will not only help you with your part of the project, but you may be able to offer input on other aspects of the project. The more you know, the more you can contribute. The more you can contribute, the more valuable you become.

Be a well-rounded employee. Know as much about your company as you can. Make yourself indispensable. If you just stick to your own defined job description, you make it harder to gain more responsibility. If you demonstrate an ability to go above and beyond your job description, however, you will get others to take notice. While it may take time, eventually you will be rewarded. You will become a better and more valuable employee. You will also be much harder to replace. If times change, your wider skill set will allow you to adapt with the times and find other jobs, if necessary.

Any pursuit can become repetitious. Poker players play different games to avoid boredom or falling into a rut. A new game offers a new perspective. This serves to keep a player fresh in his game of choice.

Avoid falling into a rut at work. Expand your horizons in order to keep yourself fresh.

No Matter What Cards You Are Dealt, You Are Not Entitled to the Pot—You Have to Earn It

A common mistake of a beginning player is to believe that he is guaranteed to win the pot when he starts with a very strong hand. I see it happen all the time. A player starts with pocket aces (two aces down) in Hold 'em, which is the strongest possible starting hand. The player then proceeds to slow play (i.e., she doesn't bet or raise) the hand in the hope of trapping some opponents and winning a big pot. The mistake with this strategy is that if you allow too many players to play, you greatly increase the chances of someone outdrawing you to a better hand. While there are certainly times to slow play a hand in order to increase your profit, you have to be very careful. A hand like pocket aces is extremely strong and an overwhelming favorite heads-up against just one other opponent. However, against a number of opponents, that same hand becomes an underdog to the other hands collectively.

Yet, time and time again, I see someone (let's call him Mr. Slow Play) slow play such a hand. Even after the flop, I will see Mr. Slow Play continue to slow play the hand, even when there are multiple players in the pot and the flop contains some cards that could allow an opponent to potentially draw out. Then, on the last card, Mr. Slow Play will come out betting hard, only to be raised by an opponent. What does Mr. Slow Play do then? Why, he re-raises, only to face another re-raise, at which point the lightbulb finally goes off in Mr. Slow Play's head, and he calls. The opponent turns over the flush, and Mr. Slow Play shows everyone his ace and complains about how unlucky he is. Mr. Slow Play is not unlucky. He is a poor poker player. He took the hand for granted and did nothing to win the pot. Mr. Slow Play had a strong hand but one that was vulnerable with a number of other opponents. He should have bet hard to knock out his opponents and either win the hand early or have only one opponent. Mr. Slow Play deserved to lose that hand and has only himself to blame for not winning it.

Take nothing for granted in life. There are no entitlements. You are not guaranteed a promotion at work just because you have been there a long time and you are next in line. You have to earn that promotion. Do everything in your power to ensure that you get it. Work longer hours. Take on more responsibility. Ask what you can do to help out others. Do more than what is required or expected. Be proactive to get what you want. Do not slow play your hand. If you are content to bide your time and wait things out, then others are sure to out-hustle you and seize the opportunity. Then, like Mr. Slow Play, you will find yourself complaining about how unjust it is when you are passed over for that promotion for someone else. Go to work every day thinking it is your last day and then work like heck to make sure it is not.

It Is Unlucky to be Superstitious

Play in any low-limit poker game and you are likely to witness one of the following scenarios. A poor player who is losing money will ask the dealer to change decks in the hope that it will change his luck. Or, when a winning player gets up and leaves, a losing player will change places and take his seat, believing that the seat is getting all of the good cards. Or you will see a losing player tell a winning player something like this: "I originally sat in that seat and then I changed my mind and moved over here."

What the losing player fails to recognize in all of these instances is that his play is responsible for his poor performance. By blaming the deck or his seat, he ignores the underlying problem. Change seats with that winning player and that winning player will still win. "It is Unlucky to be Superstitious" is a tongue-in-cheek expression. It is neither lucky nor unlucky to be superstitious. The point is that it is self-defeating to be superstitious. If you are relying on luck, you cannot succeed. Believing in superstitions distracts from the underlying task at hand. You will not play smart and hard if you believe that a rabbit's foot and a four-leaf clover have more to do with your success than your skill level.

Superstitions are self-defeating in all aspects of your life. When you rely on them, you do yourself a huge disservice. When your superstitious behaviors aren't working for you, you will have a fatalist attitude. You will believe that you cannot succeed no matter what. With that attitude, you are guaranteed not to succeed. When you perceive that the superstitions are in your favor, you may not put forth maximum effort, since you may be relying on the superstitions to carry you. If you do succeed, you will give too much credit to the superstition instead of to your skill. Rely on your skill. Do everything in your power to live up to your potential. There will be plenty of factors working against you. With hard work and smart play you can overcome them. Do not create more obstacles than you need to by introducing superstitions into your life.

ALL YOU NEED IS A CHIP AND A CHAIR

Anyone who has ever played tournament poker has heard tales of players winning a tournament after being down to their final chip. While many players think these stories are tall tales, in fact, it happens more than you would think. The most famous example is Jack Straus's incredible win at the 1982 World Series of Poker No-Limit Hold 'em Championship Event. Down to his last chip, Mr. Straus battled back from the brink of elimination to become a world champion and provide hope to every future player who found himself down to his last chip. As long as you have one chip left and a seat at the table, truly anything can happen. Yet time and time again, I see players give up when they are short-stacked in a tournament. They just throw their chips in the pot no matter what hand they're dealt, even if they have no chance to win.

As long as you are in the game, never give up. I can remember walking into a job interview years ago, and the first thing my prospective employer told me was that he had already seen a number of well-qualified candidates and had already narrowed the field down to a couple of finalists. He wanted to be upfront with me, plus I think he thought I was too young for the position. Well, as long as I had a seat in his office I was going to give it my best shot. By the end of the interview he let me know that I was one of the finalists and he wanted me to come back and meet with the manager of the company's human resources department. (I ended up declining the second interview, as the job was not an ideal fit for me, but at least I put myself in position to make that choice for myself.)

Very few things in life are final. Explore all avenues. If you are shopping for furniture and find an ideal piece that is out of your price range but has a slight nick in it, ask for money off. If the salesperson declines, ask for the department manager. If the department manager declines, ask for the store manager. If she declines, come back another day. As long as that piece of furniture is still in the store, you have a shot a getting it at a discount.

When you go on a job interview, give it your best shot from the minute you walk in until you leave the parking lot. After you leave, do not let up on the effort. Send thank-you letters to everyone you met. Make them personal and sincere by including something you talked about with each person.

If you are bidding on a project and there are other prospective buyers with higher bids than yours, you are still in the game until a contract is signed. Talk to the company about revising your bid. As long as you have a chip and a chair, you have a chance. If you do get a bid that is accepted, insist on getting a signed contract immediately, no matter what time of day it is. You want to eliminate your competition. Do not leave them with a chip and a chair.

LACK OF DISCIPLINE MAKES THE BOLD ACT FOOLISHLY

Poker requires strong, decisive action. Aggressive, bold behavior is often rewarded. In the long run, bold behavior is rewarded only when combined with discipline. Bold, aggressive action for the sake of bold, aggressive action is foolish. Bold action without discipline is not bold. It is rash and off-putting to others.

With the increasing popularity of poker, many new players try to emulate some of the more successful, aggressive players. What they do not realize is that those successful players are extremely disciplined. They use aggressive behavior when they detect an edge or sense weakness in their opponents. They take calculated risks based on reads and experience. To be aggressive just for the sake of being aggressive is foolish. The player who does not recognize this will soon be broke.

The ability to make bold decisions is an admirable quality. Look at the most successful leaders in politics, industry, and sports. I think you will find that the majority of them possess that ability. Winning football coaches will play aggressively. They will not sit on a lead. They will go for it on fourth and one when the game is on the line. They will not, however, go for it on fourth and twenty. They will punt. Winning coaches are bold but not foolish. They maintain their discipline. They run the ball to eat up the clock when they have the lead, but they are not afraid to pass when they need a first down.

Whether you are making a decision for the team at work or you are taking control of your personal finances, do your homework and learn all you can about the topic at hand. Maintain your discipline throughout the decision-making process. Then take bold, decisive action. Be willing to make a decision and take responsibility for it. Not every decision will pan out, but if every decision is made with discipline and thoughtfulness, you will soon find yourself turning into a successful and bold leader.

POKER IS A GAME OF CONTINUOUS LEARNING

Successful poker players learn something every time they play. The potential for different situations in poker is endless. No matter how experienced players are, they can always discover something new every time they play. Good players are sponges at the table. They study every hand and every player whether or not they are involved in the pot. The slightest edge in poker can make a significant difference. If you are facing a new opponent for the first time, the ability to notice one tell about a betting pattern or playing style can provide the difference between winning or losing. Poker is an easy game to learn but an extremely difficult game to master.

In just about every arena in life, those willing to put forth the effort and continue to learn are the ones who will find success. Those who think they know it all will stall out at their current level of understanding. We live in a highly specialized and competitive world. It used to be commonplace for high school children to play three or even four sports. Now the three-sports letterman is going the way of the dinosaur. Just about every sport has leagues throughout the calendar year. Areas of expertise for lawyers, accountants, doctors, engineers, and other professionals are narrowing. At the same time, there are entirely new fields that did not exist a generation ago or even a few years ago. The strides made in technology have opened up whole new professional pursuits. Even those not directly employed in those fields must have some level of understanding of them in order to compete professionally. The availability of information is now infinite. The access is instant. The workday and workweek are longer. Mobile devices allow people to stay connected to their jobs twenty-four hours a day, no matter where in the world they travel.

The pressure just to keep up can be overwhelming. Aim to do more than just keep up. Be organized, disciplined, and well balanced in your life. A healthy, fit, and well-rested body allows the mind to maximize its learning potential. Read everything. You do not have to learn it all in a day, a week, or a month. Rather, make the consistent effort throughout your life to continue learning, and you will always remain ahead of the curve.

ARE YOU A LEADER OR A FOLLOWER?

Successful poker players are leaders. Losing poker players are followers. To be a leader at the poker table is to play only those hands that you perceive give you an advantage. That advantage can be cards, position, or recognition that your opponent is vulnerable. When a leader does play a hand, she takes control of the betting. She bets or raises according to the situation to maximize her profit or chase her opponents out.

Conversely, a weak player will play hands even when he does not perceive an advantage. The weak player will often call his opponents' bets, even when his opponents have better hands. When the weak player does have a better hand, he does not bet or raise it for maximum value. Weak players often do exactly what their strong counterparts want them to do. Leaders are successful because they control the action. Followers lose money because they let the leaders control the action.

Ask yourself if you are a leader or a follower. Be honest. Life is complicated, and most people have varied interests and occupations. Life is not one-dimensional. We all have areas of strength and areas of weakness. So, more than likely, there will be areas of your life where you are a leader and areas where you are a follower. Perhaps you have always excelled at sports. Now that you are older, you coach your children's soccer and basketball teams. Having been actively involved in sports your entire life, you have great confidence in your ability to coach, lead, and teach children the fundamentals of the sport as well as sportsmanship. At work, however, you may find yourself in a new position and feel that others in your group are more knowledgeable. You tend to let others take charge and you are content to follow direction and do the best you can. Although you know that those who take charge are more likely to get favorable employee reviews and be next in line for a promotion, you lack the confidence to change the status quo. In fact, you fear that if you tried to take charge, you may only serve to expose some of your weaknesses, which will hurt your standing at work.

Certainly, there is nothing wrong with letting those who have more knowledge and confidence in a particular area take the lead in those areas. You can find contentment in doing a job well without being the leader. Participation is often a reward in and of itself. However, if you find yourself lacking fulfillment in certain areas of your life, take a closer look at those areas. I would be willing to bet (note that I am trying to control the betting here) that more often than not the area in which you lack fulfillment is an area in which you are a follower and not a leader. If that is indeed the case, take steps to correct it. Use those areas of your life where you are a leader as an example of what you can do. Expend more time and energy in the area you want to improve. Learn as much as you can. Gain the confidence necessary to be a leader. Then do it. The first time you bet in poker can be a nerve-racking experience. In hindsight, it seems incredibly simple. There is no substitute for doing. So take the first step and lead. Throw out a bet and voice your opinion. If you disagree with an opinion, raise your objection. Up the stakes and challenge yourself.

PERCEPTION IS REALITY

At the poker table, image is everything. Players go to great lengths in order to establish the right "reality." Some players play loose and aggressive early, in order to establish a reckless image. Then when they tighten up, opponents will not be able to read that they have a strong hand. Other players want everyone to fear them. They bring a huge stack to the table and talk a good game in order to intimidate their opponents. Other players will talk trash and berate opponents. Players will try all kinds of tactics in order to give themselves an advantage. The bottom line is that everyone plays with the same deck. There is no reason to be intimidated by anyone.

I remember playing in an event at the Borgata Open in September 2004. This was the same month that finals of the 2004 World Series of Poker aired on ESPN. David Williams finished second in that event. At this particular event, I was assigned to the same table as David. Before the tournament even started, some of the other players at the table were visibly in awe. They were fawning all over David. Now, of course David is an accomplished player. To be visibly intimidated, however, is self-defeating. Everyone has to play with the same deck. Yet when the tournament started, the awe carried over. I saw players scared to play against David in pots. They allowed his past success to color their judgment in this tournament.

Modesty is a great quality, but do not allow your modesty to become self-defeating. Make sure you get credit for your insightful ideas and hard work at your job. Do not step on others, but do not allow others to take credit for your contribution. Do not think that the truth will eventually come out. We all know people at work who have managed to take credit for the work of others. They have improved their reputation at the expense of others. Perception becomes reality.

We all know people who talk a big game no matter what the situation—self-proclaimed experts. Do not let allow these people to alter your reality. Judge each and every situation independently and objectively. Make your own decisions and judgments based on your observations. Have confidence in your ability and don't let someone else diminish that confidence. If you give someone more credit than he deserves, you are playing into his hand and you are operating at a disadvantage.

Above all else, project a confident image. When you speak, speak forcefully. When offering an opinion, state it proudly. When making a decision, make a choice and run with it. Do not second-guess yourself. If the decision ends up being a mistake, correct it and learn from it. If you show strength, others will perceive you as strong.

LOCATION, LOCATION, LOCATION

Everyone knows that the three most important factors to consider when looking at real estate are location, location, and location. Location is just as important at the poker table. In the great majority of games, you will win more money from the people seated to your right than you will from the people seated to your left. The reason is that you have position on those to your right. The players to your left have position on you. Having position on an opponent means that you will act after that person in most hands and thus you have an advantage.

Experienced players recognize the value of location at the table. They will scout a table out and choose a seat that they believe will maximize their expected rate of return. If they are forced to sit in an unfavorable seat, they will ask the floor manager to change tables. Or they will wait for an opponent to leave and then take her seat. Some players will even ask unsuspecting opponents to change seats with them, offering some lame excuse. What seat is the best? Some players like the weakest players to their right so they can take advantage of them all day long. Others like the hyperaggressive players to their right so they can avoid entering pots that the hyper player is playing and that are apt to be more expensive.

There really is no right answer as to what is the best seat. It is up to each player to find the seat that is ideally situated for that player's game and that will maximize his profit. What is universal is that every player should recognize the importance of location at the poker table. Each player should give as much consideration to location as every other factor in the game. Seat choice can make a big difference in a player's winnings. Players ignore it at their own peril.

Location is an instrumental factor in so many aspects of life. Two identical houses a block apart can have greatly different values based on such factors as view, noise, lot size, and topography. While everyone recognizes the value of location in real estate, there are plenty of other areas where location is important.

Office location can make a tremendous difference in your career.

If you are given a choice of offices or cubicles at work, consider location. Most of us tend to want the biggest and brightest. If we do choose location, we want to be near our friends. Next time you have a choice, consider a location that will allow you to interact on a daily basis with members of upper management. Put yourself in a position to make a positive impression on the decision makers in the office. When you enter a conference room or meeting, choose a seat that is clearly visible to everyone in the room. Make sure everyone can hear you when you offer your valuable input. Get to meetings early so you can choose location. Location can make a big difference in your success. Ignore it at your own peril.

IGNORE THE NEGATIVITY

Poker players have to have thick skin. In any game, there will be opponents who will trash talk, question your play, stare you down, and try any number of other measures to psyche you out. It is part of the game and players learn to deal with it. The solid player conditions himself to ignore all such tricks in order to concentrate on his own play and avoid revealing his own intentions. He totally shuts out both the blatant and subtle negativity emitting from his opponents.

The negativity that can affect us in the workplace is not nearly as obvious and transparent as it is at the poker table. At the office, negativity can come from any number of sources. Jealousy and fear can be overriding emotions in many people. Even those who want us to succeed may transfer their own fears upon us. This negativism can be more debilitating than that at the poker table. The negativism at the poker table is expected and thus is easy to accept and ignore. In our everyday lives when confronted with negative "vibes," our first impulse may be denial. We do not want to accept that others are negative toward us. Like the solid poker player, we must condition ourselves to detect and then ignore all of the negativism in our lives. Have your antennae up. Learn to recognize all forms of negativity from every possible source. Then shut it out. Do not let others interfere with your game plan. Be positive and concentrate on your own play, for only you know best how to proceed in your life.

NO ONE FEARS DOING THE THINGS THEY ARE TRAINED TO DO

Nothing builds confidence like experience. The first time in a poker room can be a nerve-racking experience. Even players with extensive home game or Internet experience feel nervous the first time out. Knowing the rules and etiquette and having nine strangers watching your every move takes some time to get used to. Everyone adjusts at his own rate. With experience and practice, the nerves go away. Once the nerves leave, a player can work on her game and build confidence. She will have the comfort level to try to expand her game. Soon she will not play with any fear. She will play disciplined and smart and will be doing everything in her control to maximize her profits. Of course, she will still make mistakes, but they will not be mistakes made out of fear.

Nothing in life that is worthwhile is easy. If you wish to excel at something, work hard at it. Learn everything you can and practice, practice, practice. Become an expert. Knowledge builds confidence. When you are properly trained to do a task, you will not fear or need to second-guess your work. You will make smart informed decisions. You will still make mistakes, but not like the mistakes you make when you lack skill and doubt your every move.

EXAMINE YOUR OWN PLAY

In poker, if you can figure out your opponent, you will have a tremendous advantage. All great players have an uncanny ability to read others. The great player knows his opponent's approach, whether he is weak or strong. These reads do not come without a great deal of effort. Experienced players recognize the value of reading their opponents and they put a lot of time and effort into studying and analyzing their opponents. They watch their opponents' every move and facial expressions.

As much as the great player realizes the value of knowing his opponent, he recognizes that it is only half the battle. To paraphrase Sun Tzu from *The Art of War:* "Know your opponent and know yourself and victory will be yours." Do not become so consumed with your opponents that you neglect to examine your own play. Ultimately, everything you do at the poker table should begin and end with an analysis of your own play. Your own play is the only thing you can truly control 100 percent of the time.

You should always know your competition in your industry. Know the players, their strengths and weaknesses. Study them. Learn from them. Find out their vulnerabilities. Know what they are doing and how they are doing it. Do not let them outwork, outwit, or out-will you. Do all this and excel in your job.

We all know somebody (hopefully not ourselves) who exhausts endless energy worrying about a co-worker, rival, or sworn enemy. He becomes obsessed with what this person thinks and does. He is totally consumed with what this sworn enemy thinks of him. This is extremely self-destructive behavior. It is productive and useful to study and learn from others—this provides encouragement and incentive for us to improve and grow. However, when this becomes an obsession, it is no longer productive. Our own growth and development become secondary to what this other person is doing. I see this at the poker table all the time. One player becomes so obsessed with beating another at any cost that he totally loses focus of his own play. Judgment and self-reflection go out the window. If the sworn enemy is in a hand, this guy is playing no matter what. And every single time I witness this scenario, the obsessed player loses a ton of money.

Do not be that obsessed player at work. It's not fair to your employer, the target of your obsession, or you. Study, analyze, and learn from others but keep your focus on yourself. Take care of your own development and the rest will take care of itself.

IT IS BETTER TO BE FEARED THAN LOVED

At the poker table, the ability to instill fear in your opponents is critical to your overall success. When your opponent fears you, he will be unable to play his best. He will conform his game to yours. He will play not to lose rather than play to win. He will play scared, and scared money never wins. In short, he will become so consumed with your game that he will be incapable of controlling his game.

One must be careful, however, not to incur the wrath of your opponents at the poker table. While you do not need your opponent to love you, you do not want him to hate you. You do not want to give opponents a reason to be gunning for you.

At work, you do not necessarily want to be feared, but you certainly want to be respected. You want to be strong-willed and confident. You cannot be so consumed with trying to get everyone to like you that you fail to be your own person and voice your opinion. It is much better to be respected than loved at work. Even in your private relationships, you should strive for respect. Respect begets attractions. It is much easier to like someone that you respect.

At the poker table, it is easy to put your goals of instilling fear and gaining respect ahead of being loved because everyone else at the table is your adversary. Co-workers are not adversaries. They are people who are on the same team as you. For each member of the team to contribute, he must feel free to express himself. He must have the respect of his teammates in order to be heard and taken seriously. However, in close relationships at work, the goal of gaining respect sometimes takes a backseat to wanting to be loved. You can have both.

HIGHER AMBITIONS LEAD TO HIGHER SUCCESS

In tournament poker, you typically find players with varying degrees of ambition. First, there are the players who are just happy to be there. Next, you have those players whose primary goal is to make it to the money. (By way of example, in a tournament of two hundred people, usually the top twenty players will make money. However, as noted earlier, there will be a huge difference in the amount of money the first-place finisher makes compared to that of the twentieth-place finisher.) Finally, you have those players who want to win it all. In tournament poker, you have to balance the two competing goals of chip accumulation and survival. Those players with lower ambitions will emphasize survival. Those players with higher ambitions will go after the chips—they will play to win.

You only live once—play to win. Do not be content to just survive and get by in your pursuits. Shoot for the stars. Even if you miss, you will still do a lot better than if your only goal is to get by. The higher your ambitions, the higher your successes will be.

FOCUS, FOCUS, FOCUS

Sometimes you can find an edge in the tiniest of details. As a corporate lawyer, I have been trained to pay strict attention to the most minute of details. When drafting or reviewing documents, you must construct or read every sentence carefully. The insertion or deletion of one word can dramatically change the meaning of the provision. Often, a sentence can be read more than one way. That is why it is critical to double-check everything and, if you have the manpower, have an extra pair of eyes review the work. It is always good to get a fresh perspective.

My training as a lawyer has served me well at the poker table. I pay attention to everything. There can be many distractions in a poker room. There are usually televisions posted around the room, waitresses serving drinks and food, lots of noise, and a crowd of viewers at high stakes games. Many inexperienced players take a look at their cards and decide whether or not to play. If they decide not to play, they fold their cards and wait for the next hand. The experienced player watches everyone else when the cards are dealt. He waits until it his turn to act before he even looks at his cards. What everyone has done before him will greatly determine how he plays. This player is paying attention to every detail, not just his cards. If he does fold, he continues to study the actions of his opponents. If he plays, he studies his opponents as the new cards are dealt. He can always look at his own cards later. The one bit of information you can review at any time is your own cards. Yet, most inexperienced players will choose to look at this first. This is a mistake. Watching your opponents' reaction to their cards is information you can only get in a quick second. Why be reviewing your cards when they are looking at theirs? Your cards are not going anywhere. You can look at your cards in a few moments. You never know when you will find that one bit of information that will give you an edge. The good player who keeps his focus on the game and on his opponents, avoiding other distractions, is likely to find that well-hidden edge.

No matter what the task, stay focused on the job. You never know where you will find that edge. Avoid any distractions. Be totally committed to the task, and I guarantee that if there is a hidden edge, you will be the one to find it. Once achieved, ask a trusted co-worker or friend to review your work. A fresh perspective can be invaluable. Use every available resource to help you maintain and refine your focus. You should make it a goal in life to never lose out on anything due to a lack of focus.

SOME DAYS YOU ARE THE PIGEON AND SOME DAYS YOU ARE THE STATUE

We all have good days and bad days. In poker, the differences can be extreme due to the capriciousness of the cards. There will be sessions when you can do no wrong. The cards all go your way. Your strong hands hold up when you bet them and get three callers. When you are on a draw, the deck always brings that fifth spade that you need. If you have a monster hand, at least one other opponent will have a very strong hand and pay you off. At the end of the day, you will be up a lot of money.

On the flip side, there will be sessions when nothing goes your way. Your strong hands will lose to some joker calling with two outs who happens to hit his miracle card on the river. When your first four cards are spades, you never get the fifth one. When you finally do get a very strong hand, you are up against a monster. In fact, all day you get a lot of second-best hands and lose a lot of money.

Nonetheless, in the long run, skill wins out in poker. Experienced players know that poker can be a very "streaky" game and they learn not to get too high when things are going well or too low when things are running bad. As long as their play remains solid, they know that they will be successful over time.

Very few pursuits in life are a sprint. Your first job out of college isn't going to be as chief executive officer of a Fortune 500 company. Success is measured over a long period of time, and along the way there will be many peaks and valleys. Learn to keep them all in perspective. Enjoy your successes, but try not to let them go to your head or allow yourself to rest on your laurels. If you receive praise for a project well done at work, share that praise with other members of the team.

Conversely, do not get too down when you suffer setbacks. If your boss is having a bad day and unfairly criticizes you for something a co-worker did, correct the problem rather than complaining. You can let it be known that you weren't responsible but only in the same breath that you offer a solution. Be proactive and keep your play solid. As long as your play remains solid, the good days and bad days will come and go, but over the long run, your success will be ensured.

THE POKER EXPERIENCE

Sweating the Magician

On the heels of the success of my first poker book, Tournament Poker and the Art of War, *I was hired by the World Poker Tour to cowrite the next book in their highly successful series. The main authority on the book was a top professional poker player, Antonio "the Magician" Esfandiari. I had played in tournaments with Antonio but did not know him personally. My job was to work with him to get all of his thoughts, ideas, and strategies down on paper in a coherent and entertaining way.*

I arranged a trip to Las Vegas during the 2005 World Series of Poker (WSOP) to meet and spend some time with Antonio both at and away from the tables. This was the first year that the WSOP would be held at the Rio convention center, and it was quite a spectacle. There were over two hundred tables spread throughout the cavernous room running twenty-four hours a day. Each day leading up to the main event had one or two specific preliminary tournament events, as well as numerous satellite tournaments and a slew of cash games. Depending on what events were running, Antonio would either be playing in a tournament or in a cash game. Since the focus of our book was to be on cash games, we planned for me to come out there when he would be playing those games.

The instant I met Antonio, I knew the book was going to be a success. Not only is he a great player, Antonio is personality personified. He immediately made me feel at home and was a gracious host. He introduced me around the table, and we got to work. He was in the middle of a game, and I sat down behind him to sweat him. In poker terminology, to sweat a player is to sit behind him and follow his every move so you can learn how he plays. The player being sweated will show his cards to the observer and explain some of his actions. Of course, many players are justifiably unwilling to share this much information with anyone. Others will share only with close friends or players that they are tutoring. In this case, Antonio's sharing made sense, since I would be working with him on the book.

I started out taking detailed notes on Antonio's moves and strategies. I asked a lot of questions about different situations and philosophies to get information beyond the hands I observed. After a while, my focus changed from learning Antonio's strategy to watching him work. This was his job, after all.

I was in Antonio's office and I was impressed at how he plied his craft. Well before he became a professional poker player, Antonio was an accomplished magician. You could see the entertainer in him. He worked the table, the room, and his cards seamlessly. Whether he was talking to a poker peer or a wealthy amateur trying his luck, Antonio knew just what to say to lead the conversation and the action.

The opportunities that are available to poker players now would have been unheard of a few short years ago. Books, DVDs, television exposure, and endorsements are available. There are more great players, though, than there are endorsement deals. It was no coincidence that Antonio was chosen to author the World Poker Tour book. He sells himself. Poker in Las Vegas is a modern-day phenomena, and Antonio is at the vortex. While he is playing, he attracts attention from professionals, fans, and hangers-on. During the first couple of hours I was there, he was approached for pictures, autographs; someone even asked for his assistance in getting on the guest list for a hot new nightclub. Antonio obliged them all with an upbeat, carefree demeanor. Meantime, he was still playing high stakes no-limit Texas Hold 'em at a table with two former world champions (Greg Raymer and Phil Helmuth Jr.). When I play for much lower stakes, I never take my eyes off the action or players at the table. However, Antonio never missed a beat, and when we broke for a late dinner, he was comfortably ahead.

The next morning I received a text message from Antonio that he was at the Rio. I headed over and found him eating breakfast and having a cup of coffee with Phil Laak and Jennifer Tilley. They were there for ESPN's taping of the Roshambo championships. Roshambo is the official name for that classic childhood game Rock, Paper, Scis-

sors. Antonio, I found out, is not a Roshambo expert, but the event was being covered by ESPN.

Later that same day, I was searching the Amazon room for Antonio when I heard a friendly voice yell, "Dr. Dave, over here." Antonio has a way of making everyone feel welcome with his addition of the prefix "Dr." I turned my head to find out that "over here" was the main stage of the World Series. Since there was no final table being filmed at the moment, ESPN was filming Antonio performing various card and chip tricks. I came over to watch. Antonio was performing trick after trick and then watching the replay in slow motion in the monitor. He had a tremendous camaraderie with the producers, and it was obvious that they loved him.

At that moment, I realized that this is not a job for Antonio, this is a career. Poker may not stay this popular forever, but Antonio is making the most of the opportunity. I have heard plenty of other successful poker players complain of their lack of endorsements. Antonio has more than his fair share because he goes after it. He plays every angle. He gets involved and makes himself a pleasure to be around. As I walked through the Rio that night to dinner with Antonio, he was stopped by young girls, older men, young guns of poker, and older women. Everyone wanted to shake his hand or get a picture with him. No one was disappointed. Antonio is one of the most marketable poker players in the world because not only is he a good player, he has an innate underlying business savvy. He really gets it.

7. TOP PAIR: HOW SUCCESSFUL POKER PLAYERS AND BUSINESSPEOPLE THINK

I'm routinely asked poker questions such as "How should I play A-K in late position?" or "What kind of raise should I make with pocket jacks under the gun?" My answer to these questions and just about every other poker question posed to me is "It depends." That's not meant to be a coy response. In fact, I will often ask a number of qualifying questions to dig deeper—my ultimate goal is helping the inquirer understand the complexity of all the different factors that go into making a correct decision at the poker table.

Poker—no matter what the form—is a very situational game. Every game and hand is unique. How you play depends on a whole slew of factors including, to name a few, the number of opponents, the nature of your opponents, your position, what has transpired previously, the cards you're holding, and the size of the respective chip stacks. Strategic questions can't be considered in a vacuum. Poker, like the world at large, does not work that way.

To win at poker you need to exercise good judgment. You study as much as you can about the game. Read books on it. Discuss strategy with trusted friends and other players. Replay hands in your mind and dissect what you did right and wrong. The kinds of situations you can face are endless, so you never stop learning. As you gain more knowledge and experience, your judgment improves. When faced with a new situation, you will be able to rely on a lifetime of experience and knowledge to make increasingly more correct decisions.

Poker is fluid. The game changes quickly. The style of play today is vastly different than it was five years ago. The good players aren't stuck in their ways. They keep up with the changing dynamics.

The business world is also an ever-changing environment. The technological changes accelerate over time as new technology builds on old technology. Business leaders are not afraid of change. The good ones don't ignore it. They embrace it. They read as much as possible. They network. They soak up as much information as possible and discuss strategy with others. They never stop learning. If they do, they will lose.

There are no absolutes in the business world. One can only rely on her wealth of experience and knowledge to make the correct decision. You can't wait for a sure thing. You have to trust your judgment based on research and go with it. It's a lot easier to trust your judgment, however, if you have been open to learning and doing everything in your power to gain knowledge and experience.

I started playing a home poker game a few years back. We had just moved into a new construction neighborhood, and one of the men in the community wanted to start a biweekly poker night. I had very low expectations of the quality of poker to be played but figured it was a great way to make some new friends and to get to know some of the neighbors. My expectations were met on both accounts.

The majority of the players had very little, if any, understanding of poker. The few who were familiar with poker knew nothing in the way of any advanced strategy. We were playing just for fun with no money at stake, so the entire purpose was to socialize. The conversations had little to do with poker and a lot to do with our jobs, families, and the neighborhood.

After a few months, a couple of new neighbors joined, and we started playing a no-limit Hold 'em tournament for small stakes. I won just about every time I played that first year. I had been upfront about my poker experience since day one and was not the one who suggested playing for money. In fact, I was uncomfortable playing for money with my neighbors and I advocated keeping the stakes low. Still, if I was going to play, I was going to play to win. It's the only way I know.

I didn't offer any unsolicited advice but was more than happy to share as much knowledge as I could with anyone who asked. A couple of the newer guys would ask questions all the time and even read a few of my books. In a short time, they easily surpassed most of the other players who were content to just show up on Friday nights. They made such big improvements because they wanted to learn. They could have easily found another source (there's plenty of good poker strategy books on the market) for their information, but I was ready, willing, and able to help and made myself easily accessible.

After a few more months of playing, I invited the group to the Trump Taj Mahal Casino in Atlantic City, where I was one of the featured authors in the first annual Poker Author's Challenge no-limit Hold 'em tournament. Four of the regulars made it, and for each of them, it was their first tournament outside of our home game. Two of the four were players who had asked me a lot of questions and read a few of my books. The other two rarely asked questions and seemed less interested when I tried to offer some advice. There were over two hundred entries in the tournament. The two players who asked fewer questions went out fairly quickly. The other two, however, advanced very far. One finished in nineteenth place, just one place out of the money. The other finished in fourth place, which was a fantastic finish in a fairly competitive event.

The experience of this event seemed to energize our home game. More players started joining, the stakes were raised a little bit, and the games became more competitive. While I still won more than my fair share, I was by no means guaranteed a victory. Nearly everyone asked a lot of questions. About six months after the Author's Tournament, a group of nine from our home game went to the Borgata Casino in Atlantic City to play in their Sunday tournament. Six of the nine were playing in their first-ever tournament in a casino. The other three had only the Author's Tournament under their belt. (I did not make it.)

Their results were outstanding by any measure. Four of the nine finished in the top eleven of the entire tournament. Their respective finishes were eleventh, tenth, fifth, and first. It was a real testament to the desire to learn and get better. Now, none of these guys was ready to hit the poker circuit full time, but that wasn't their goal in the first place. These were recreational players who wanted to improve their play and be competitive in that environment. They had admirably met that goal. No matter what your interests are or whether you're doing something as a career or a hobby, you'll only get out of it what you put in to it.

WHEN THE CARDS ARE RUNNING BAD

At work and in your private life, get things done well before deadlines. You can never foresee all of the things that could possibly go wrong, so give yourself a cushion. Every problem has a solution, but it may take time to find it. We're all human. If things in our private lives are hectic, they are bound to spill over and affect our concentration and time at work. You never know when problems will arise. In poker, it's usually when you're short on money that you get blindsided by that runner—runner flush and lose a monster pot. If you hadn't squandered money earlier, you would perhaps have been better prepared to handle that loss.

When bad luck happens, do not go on tilt. Do not become defeatist. Accept the challenge. Remain positive and deal with it the best that you can. No matter how hard you try and how prepared you are, things won't always go your way. You can exercise excellent judgment and still lose.

Most people can perform well when things are running well. It's how you play when the cards are running badly that separates the winners from the losers. The biggest difference between winners and losers in every venue in life is how they handle adversity. Good players bounce back from losses. Good businesses rise to meet new challenges.

THE BOTTOM LINE IS HOW MUCH YOU WIN

At the end of the day in poker, you are judged by one thing and one thing only—how much you win or lose. You are either up or down. In poker the results are tangible, and it is very easy to keep score. However, poker is a fickle game. Sometimes you can do everything right but win. Win or lose, after every poker session, you should take the time to examine your play and see where you can improve. If you do not learn something every time you play, you will not be successful. Because of the capricious nature of poker, success must be measured over the long term. Short-term gains and losses should be taken with a grain of salt. If you concentrate on the process and how well you are playing, the end result should take care of itself over the long term.

There is nothing wrong with winning in life. Do not feel guilty about any of your successes. Winning comes from hard work and perseverance. In the majority of cases, those who win in life have earned it.

POKER IS A GAME OF ADJUSTMENTS

To be successful in poker, you must constantly make adjustments. Good starting hands can go south in a hurry. Very strong hands can lose to monster hands. Weak starting hands can have value if you have position or are playing against malleable opponents. A hand of poker changes with every card, every bet, every action or inaction. Furthermore, since poker is a game of imperfect information, you may not necessarily know how the hand has changed. You must use all of your experience and instincts to make split-second decisions to the best of your ability. In poker, there have been plenty of times that I have been ready to make a big bet when the player before me beats me to the punch. Now I must completely reevaluate my position. Is he bluffing? Is my hand not as strong as I think it is in this situation? Or has this player just played into my strength?

Life also is about constant change. However, unlike poker, the changes are typically not as rapid. This has its plusses and minuses. In poker, the good player knows the changes are coming fast and furious and she is always on guard to react to them. In life, the changes are often more gradual. Thus, it takes more work and effort to recognize them. In business, jobs that are in demand today may be outsourced next year. A good investment in today's market may be a poor one down the road. Nothing is static. A blue chip company may slowly become irrelevant as your investment dwindles. However, by the time you realize that the company is becoming a dinosaur, the damage is already done.

The good thing about life changes is that you usually have more time to react to them than in poker. (Even an unexpected pregnancy offers nine months of preparation.) If you realize that life is about constant change, then you are ahead of the game. You can train yourself to stay attuned to those changes that affect you and your investments. Changes in technology that seem to happen overnight are actually years in the making. By reading as much as you can and gaining knowledge, you can learn to foresee the coming trends. While no one can accurately predict the future, anyone can arm himself with as much knowledge as possible to make an educated guess.

KNOW THE FUNDAMENTALS OF PLAY BUT DO NOT ALWAYS PLAY BY THE BOOK

No matter what you are pursuing in life, you should become as knowledgeable as you can on the subject. Poker is no different. In order to be successful, one must know the fundamentals of the game inside and out. That is, one must know which hands are playable in which situations. Additionally, players should have a thorough understanding of how to calculate the odds of winning in just about every situation, so they can accurately judge how to play any given situation. Armed with the fundamentals, most players will probably be able to hold their own against equal or lesser opponents. They will play the hands and fold the hands that they should. They will bet, raise, check, and fold according to the standards of play. However, if these players always play by the book, there will be a ceiling on how far they can go. Their play will be predictable, something an astute opponent will be more than ready to take advantage of.

Most pursuits in life are similar to poker. While a clear understanding of the fundamentals is essential, more is needed to ensure success. If you are writing a novel, you must start out with a complete understanding of the basic structure and how it works. However, most successful fiction authors will depart from that structure in order to make their work stand out and be unpredictable. Some will experiment to the point that the underlying structure is barely recognizable. An aspiring writer may think he does not need to learn the fundamentals. That would be a big mistake. You must know the rules before you can decide how they can be bent or broken.

Successful poker players mix up their play, keep it unpredictable, and are always thinking two steps ahead. They look at the entire situation and try to determine what opportunities are there to exploit. They know what their opponent is likely to be thinking and they play off of that.

No matter what you are pursuing, soak up as much information as you can on the subject. Then try to gather information on ancillary or tangential topics that may provide additional insights on your subject. For example, if you have designed a new children's T-shirt that you want to sell locally, you should gather as much information as you can about that market. Who carries children's clothing, whom do they buy from, and what are their terms of payment are just a few of the questions you should find answers to first. Next, find out about other commercial enterprises in the area. Perhaps a children's entertainment center that does not sell clothing would let you set up a kiosk inside the center. Put yourself in the mind of other sellers of merchandise. What would they do? Find out and then try to think of ways you can outsell them. Be creative. Think of ways to push the boundaries of traditional methods in order to give yourself an edge.

LOOK FOR A REASON TO FOLD

You can't bluff a sucker because he looks for any reason to call. Conversely, good players look for a reason to fold. The good player views her opponents with a critical eye. She is wary of traps. She does not have anything to prove to anyone. Her one and only goal is to make money and she realizes that the chips you do not lose are as important as the chips you win. Sure, she can be bluffed at times, but that is because she is no sucker. There will be few times when she pays off her opponents by playing a hand that she should not play. She is not careless with her chips. She can remain objective and emotionally detached from the game. She plays with a purpose, not to feel empowered. She recognizes that she is defined not by the cards she is dealt but rather by how she plays them. She knows that even the worst players will get their fair share of cards. The good player does not play hands when she has the worst of it. Rather, she waits until she perceives an advantage—whether it is cards, position, or weakness in her opponents—and then exploits that advantage. She does not squander chips playing into other people's strengths. Rather, she saves them to back her own strengths. She does not chase hands. Sure, she will miss out on a few winning hands, but she will save a heck of a lot of losing hands.

In your everyday life, look for reasons to fold. If you are an impulsive buyer, look for reasons not to make your next purchase. Be skeptical. Ask yourself why you are buying this item. Write down every reason why you should not buy this product. Does this purchase play into your strengths or the seller's?

Do not blindly follow the next stock tip your friend offers you. Do your own research. Be critical of the company and its stock valuation. Brainstorm about everything that can go wrong with the company. Set up tough standards and follow through only on those tips that satisfy your new standards. Make investments only when you perceive an advantage. Do not squander your chips when you cannot adequately articulate your advantage.

In looking at prospective employers, be picky if you can afford to be. The interview process is a give and take. Be honest and forthcoming with any questions asked of you. However, you should ask probing questions of your interviewers. As long as it is done in a professional manner, prospective employers will respect and admire tough questions from their candidates. For instance, you might ask whether the company has been profitable for each of the last three years and whether earnings are increasing and at what rate.

Do not feel the need to jump at every business opportunity that comes your way. You do not have to take advantage of every one. Sure, you may miss out on a few winners, but you will avoid a lot of losers.

Do not waste your chips needlessly. My wife has taught me the value of smart shopping. I used to be a sucker for a sale. I would buy a shirt because it was inexpensive, not because I liked it. Then I would never wear it because I did not like it. Where is the value in that? Now I ask myself if I am really going to wear the item before making a purchase. I still shop in the discount bin, but I look for a reason to fold.

POKER IS A GAME OF IMPERFECT INFORMATION

The essence of poker is that at any given time, each player is privy to some information but not all of the information. If a player could somehow see her opponents' cards, the game would certainly open up for her. She would know exactly where her cards stood in relation to her opponents' cards. More important, she would have great insight into how her opponents felt about their hands and use that to her advantage. Fortunately, players do not have X-ray vision, and so the essence of poker remains preserved. Players must use their experience and skill in order to ascertain what cards their opponent may hold. Good players will test their opponents. That is, they will bet or raise their opponent in order to see how he reacts. How the opponent reacts may reveal insight into the strength of that opponent's hand. Sometimes, however, a player has no choice but to call bets all the way to the river in order to find out what his opponent is holding.

Fortunately, life does not have to be a game of imperfect information. In today's technologically advanced world, an endless amount of information on practically any topic is just a mouse click away. Buying a new car? There are plenty of Web sites that can provide invoice price, sticker price, and average selling price in your area. Shopping for furniture? Then do your comparison shopping on the Internet. You can visit dozens of stores in minutes—a task that would have been impossible ten years ago. Looking to refinance? Again, every mortgage option and accompanying rates are easily accessible. Looking to invest in the stock of a promising company? Analyst reports, SEC filings, financial information, and earnings projections are all readily available for any publicly traded company.

There is no excuse in today's world to enter any transaction with your eyes half shut. Be proactive and make yourself as knowledgeable as possible. Every card is face up if you look hard enough for it.

AVOID ATTRIBUTING YOUR OWN BEHAVIOR TO EXTERNAL CAUSES

Weak players tend to attribute their bad results to bad luck. They refuse to take responsibility for their own mistakes. As we've seen, they blame the dealer, the cards, the seat, and anything else they can think of but themselves. Conversely, when they are winning due to luck, they attribute this to internal causes. They believe their skill and cunning are responsible for their hitting that miracle card on the river to win a big pot.

The biggest strength a good poker player has is the ability to objectively analyze his own play. He recognizes when he is playing well and when he is playing poorly. He knows when he has just lucked out or when he has earned a pot. Being objective is the only way to improve as a player. As easy a concept as this is to understand, it is an extremely difficult concept to put into practice—especially for the beginning player. Every player has an ego. We all like to think we have skill. For the player who dominates his neighborhood game and then walks into a casino, the experience can be a humbling one. It is human nature not to admit fault. With such a huge luck factor in poker, there are plenty of ready-made excuses. It is just way too easy to attribute losses to external causes. It takes real guts to look internally.

Be accountable for your actions in real life. With accountability comes improvement. Without accountability, expect continued mediocrity and failure. Have guts and look inward rather than outward. Whenever anything bad happens in your life, make it a habit to look to yourself first. There will certainly be plenty of times when things are not your fault. However, if you train yourself to look inward first, you will be less likely to blame external causes. Only after you objectively eliminate yourself from fault should you begin to look at external causes. There are plenty of ready-made excuses in the world. Avoid using them. Go through every possible scenario of what you could have done before blaming external forces. Not only will you learn and correct your behavior, you will earn the respect of your peers, friends, and family.

When things are going well, take the time to understand the cause. Is your skill responsible or are some external forces at work? During the boom market of the late 1990s, plenty of investors falsely believed they had the Midas touch. Of course, we all know now that the "irrational exuberance" of the market was responsible for the runaway stock prices, not some special ability on our part to pick stocks that would exponentially rise over the short term.

The good poker player looks to minimize and control external causes. When a player gets eliminated from a poker tournament and says, "I was card dead; I just couldn't get anything to play with," it drives me nuts. Winning players create opportunities. They don't always rely on their cards to win pots. I guarantee that at some point in that tournament, that griping player had an opportunity to win some chips that he did not take advantage of. He could have used his position or attacked his opponents when they were vulnerable or he could have set up some tricky bluffs. Not everything you try is going to work, but the point is that if you're not getting cards, you have to try something. You can't let external causes dictate your destiny.

Good leaders don't look for excuses, no matter how ready-made they are. Those external causes become obstacles to overcome and not the path to defeat. If your subordinate isn't doing the job, maybe he's not getting proper guidance from you. If your boss is never satisfied, maybe you're not performing to expectations. If other departments or outside third parties aren't giving your ideas the respect you believe they deserve, then maybe you're not communicating your message effectively. Don't blame external causes, try to control and master them.

AVOID ATTRIBUTING YOUR OPPONENTS' BEHAVIOR TO EXTERNAL CAUSES

Just as weak players tend to attribute their bad results to bad luck, they are quick to attribute their opponents' good play to good luck. This is a big mistake. Rather than adjust their play in order to better compete, they easily dismiss their opponents' success. Conversely, when an opponent suffers bad luck, the weak player is quick to attribute the loss to internal causes. He wants to believe that his opponent is inferior. By doing this, he feeds right into his opponent's strength. He will continue to challenge his opponent, believing that his luck has to turn around. If the opponent is a strong player, he will use this to easily manipulate the weak player. The strong opponent will play hands only when he has the advantage, knowing that the weak player will pay him off.

Do not underestimate people in your everyday life. Give them the proper respect that they deserve. If you underestimate people's ability, you will find yourself woefully underprepared. Your first assumption should always be that someone earned his way in life. When you make this assumption, you will force yourself to prepare properly. You will work that much harder in order to effectively compete. If you are wrong about your original assumption, so be it. You have still gained by bettering yourself. To belittle another's accomplishments or attribute those accomplishments to luck or external causes is self-defeating. You are telling yourself that you need luck to get ahead in this world, so what is the sense in trying.

Leaders never underestimate the competition even if they are comfortably ahead of them. Others can always improve through hard work and determination. Even if you're ahead of the game, never ease up and dismiss a gain by your opponent as just a lucky move.

Do Not Fall in Love with Your Cards

Nothing clouds a player's judgment more than great cards. There's a rush of adrenaline as dreams turn toward scooping a big pot. The question isn't *if* I'm going to win but *how much* I'm going to win. Ask any player what her favorite hand is, and she may have an amusing anecdote about how she won a big pot with jack-five suited—so that's now her favorite hand. But ask any player what hand she wants to receive at crunch time, and her answer will always be pocket aces. Every time you see two of those big aces staring at you in your hand, there's an instant attraction. You'll fall in love every time.

Those aces aren't going to win every time, however. If you want to succeed, you're going to have to occasionally make the tough break with those aces. To do that, you have to be objective and remain emotionally detached. Don't fall in love in the first place. Aces are the strongest possible starting hand, but if you find yourself in trouble after the flop, you have to get rid of them. It's a lot easier to part ways with cards you feel indifferent about.

Businesspeople know that they will get the best results if they remain objective throughout a transaction. You can be ambitious, passionate, and strong willed. You can feel extremely confident about the prospects of a deal. You can't, however, fall in love with it. Retain your objectivity. Often, the best deals are the ones that are not made. Wanting to do a deal at any cost will inevitably cost you a great deal.

Pocket aces look great on the surface, but there are still five cards to come that can change the outlook dramatically. Things change. More research or due diligence can reveal new problems. Adversaries may surprise you with new wrinkles in the negotiations. The process of going through the motions in a potential transaction may lead to a discovery about your own business, which may lead you in a new direction. If you haven't fallen in love with the deal, it won't hurt so much to break it off.

WHAT ABOUT DECEPTION?

Deception is an integral part of any poker game. Players must both know how to implement deception and recognize it when implemented by an opponent. The ability to do both is a skill—innate in some, learned by others. There are no ethical considerations when it comes to deception in poker. Deception is both accepted and expected. Poker is a truly Darwinian exercise. Players can use any trick at their disposal (outside of cheating, which is, of course, unethical and expressly prohibited) to trip up, trap, or deceive their opponents. The good player knows how to make a timely bluff in order to induce an opponent to fold a winning hand. Or the good player can hide the strength of his own hand in order to maximize the profit he wins from an unsuspecting opponent.

What role does deception play in the world outside of poker? While the art of deception is an admirable skill in the poker room, it is generally not desirable in just about any other context. This does not mean that the skill is without merit in the real world. Rather, the skill must be implemented within the ethical boundaries of the arena in which you are operating. Little white lies to spare feelings allow one to be diplomatic. The ability to smooth over mistakes can save your company from embarrassment. In negotiations, it is certainly acceptable to temper your enthusiasm for getting a deal done in order to maintain bargaining power. Even bluffing is acceptable if you are willing to live with the consequences. That is, if you state a position as "take it or leave it," and your opponent chooses to call your bluff and "leave it," then you must live with the decision or lose all credibility if you subsequently back off your position.

The skill set required in poker that also comes in handy in the real world is the ability to detect deception. Unfortunately, while ethical boundaries exist in all areas, far too many people do not follow them. These unethical players treat the real world like the poker room. They believe that anything they can get away with is fair game. Many professionals are trained to detect deception. Traders in financial markets are trained to spot market manipulation when markets move one way or another. Negotiators look for tells and negotiating patterns to detect when their adversaries are bluffing.

Fortunately, you do not need to be a professional to detect deception. Adopt a poker playing mentality to help weed out the lies and deceit of others. If you have ever hung around a poker room, you have probably heard some players make a statement along the lines of "I have to keep you honest," and then they call with a marginal hand. The point of this kind of call is that you don't want to allow an opponent to keep bluffing you out of a hand.

When I suspect a player is playing a little too fast and loose with his cards, I'll make what I call a "probe bet" to find out information. I'll raise him and put the pressure back on him to see if he really has the cards or not. I find it less costly to make the occasional probe bet than to sit around waiting for good cards. If he's bluffing, he's going to fold rather than call and show his bluff. Even if I guess wrong, I've sent the message that I'm going to "keep him honest," and he'll usually slow down his play against me.

In the business world, there are many ways to make probe bets. Ask for references up front and contact them. Make sure they have plenty of experience in the kind of work required of them. Test a supplier or vendor out with a small project before committing to a larger one. Hold enough money back until the job is completed. Periodically, check in on the progress. Stay hands-on and monitor the work of the project or hire a third party to monitor. Don't be shy about asking for more information or proof of the claims that they are making. It's nothing personal, it's just business.

At the poker table, you have to adopt the mentality that you are going to steal your best friend's money through whatever deceptive means you can. Your friend is going to understand that, without any hard feelings, and he will do whatever he needs to do to protect himself. After all, it's not personal, it's just poker. While the ethics in the business world are very different, the fact that it's not personal remains the same. No one should have any objection to your making some "probe bets" to try to protect yourself.

SIT IN YOUR OPPONENT'S CHAIR— AND PLAY HIS CHIPS, TOO

I see the following situation all the time in poker. An otherwise tight player (let's call her Ms. B) makes a big bet with a weak hand when she knows her opponent has a mediocre hand. Ms. B believes that her tight image will buy her some respect, especially when her opponent has a very marginal hand. To Ms. B's surprise, her opponent calls. Well, if Ms. B had been paying attention, she would have realized that her opponent was calling bets all night with marginal hands. In fact, this opponent had a tough time laying down any mediocre hand. The mistake Ms. B made is, in fact, a fairly common one. She projected her own frame of reference onto her opponent. Ms. B correctly put herself in her opponent's position. She put herself right there in her opponent's chair and imagined what it would be like to face the decision her opponent would face. Ms. B's mistake, however, was to answer the question herself rather than how her opponent would have answered. To understand her opponent, Ms. B needed to not only understand her opponent's position but also how her opponent would react. In other words, Ms. B needed to not only put herself in her opponent's chair but play her opponent's chips as her opponent would.

It is very hard to get away from our own frame of reference. We assume we have a very logical way of thinking and a fair amount of common sense. When we imagine how others would react in a certain situation, we all think we can easily put ourselves in our opponents' shoes. When thinking how our opponent would react in that situation, however, most of us will project our own thoughts and feelings onto our opponent. This is a big mistake. What we should be doing is trying to determine how our opponent thinks. We must imagine what he would do in that situation completely independent of what we would do.

Take a minute to think of all the crazy things people you know have done. Now think of things that friends have done that may not be so crazy but still were not how you would have done them. Now think of somebody who you think is very similar to you. Think of someone who shares your beliefs and values. Now think how different you are from that person. Think of your different opinions, likes, and dislikes. The point of this exercise is to show how very different we all are. Therefore, to really understand someone else's position requires a lot more than putting yourself in his shoes. You must also think as he would think and not as you would think.

When you practice this exercise at the poker table, the entire game opens up. You can anticipate the likely next move of your opponents and recognize their vulnerabilities. You'll know when you should attack and when you should retreat. Knowing yourself and maintaining self-control is only half the battle. The ability to understand your opponents allows you to master the game.

Negotiation becomes so much easier when you can grasp the other side's motives, desires, and fears. Find common ground where possible, push your advantage in areas where there is vulnerability, and compromise on issues sensitive to both sides.

THE POKER EXPERIENCE

Finding Answers in Other Disciplines

I have been playing poker for over twenty-five years and I started playing tournament poker seriously in 1999. Living only ninety minutes from Atlantic City, my brother-in-law Jim and I used to take monthly trips to the Tropicana during the late 1990s. This was still a few years before the poker boom. The waiting lists were short, most of the tables were set up for seven-card stud, and all of the Hold 'em tables were limit.

Back then the Tropicana and the Taj Mahal were the only casinos in Atlantic City that had poker rooms of any decent size. The Tropicana was the only casino to offer regular weekly poker tournaments. The Taj had the US Poker Championships once a year, but that was it.

On one of our trips, we decided to play a tournament. The offering that night was seven-card stud. I lasted about halfway through the tournament before I was essentially anted out. I enjoyed the contest, though. Going forward, we planned our monthly excursions around the tournament schedule. I played a few more seven-card stud tournaments with the same result. I lasted long enough to get a taste of tournament play but did not even sniff the money. At first, I blamed my losses on the fast structure and bad cards. I was making the classic tournament beginner's mistakes. I was playing the tournament as if it were a cash game and then placing blame on everything but my own play. I thought you had to have a lot of luck to advance. However, after just a few tournaments, I saw some familiar faces making the money every time. For the first time, I began to look inside. Maybe it wasn't just the cards that were holding me back. Maybe my play was fundamentally flawed.

I decided I had to make a change. I went home and read Sun Tzu's The Art of War. *Actually, I should state that I reread the book. During my first week on the job at my old Wall Street law firm, one of the senior partners took me aside and told me that the two books every attorney should read are* Sun Tzu's The Art of War *and Machiavelli's* The Prince. *I took the message to heart and have never regretted it. Both of those books offer some incredible wisdom that has widespread application. I had always applied these teachings to the corporate world but had yet to truly incorporate them into my poker playing in a real in-depth manner.*

After rereading The Art of War *with a critical eye toward poker, I thought this was a manual for poker tournaments. I should not be acting until I had an edge. I should be maximizing that edge. I should be exploiting weaknesses in my opponents. Everyone played with the same deck, so they could not be getting good cards all of the time either. I had been playing not to lose. I was afraid of being eliminated, so I hung onto my tournament chips for dear life. I had to retool. Instead of calling off chips only to give them up, I had to use those chips to push others off or get them to call when I had the best hand. Most important, I had to act when my chips still had some power. If I allowed myself to get short-stacked, I was sure to be attacked. I had to make a move while I could still be a force. Any fool can play conservatively and advance to the middle of the field before being anted or blinded out (posting the mandatory blinds and antes and thus losing your chip stack). If you wanted to win, you had to constantly be thinking ahead and accumulating chips for the next level. Soon, I could not wait to play my next tournament.*

There was one catch, however. I believed that the harnessing and use-of-force principles learned from The Art of War *would have more meaning applied in an arena where there was no limitation on the amount of force you could unleash at any time. Fortunately for me, such an arena existed—no-limit Hold 'em tournaments. I decided to switch gears and apply my newfound knowledge to a no-limit Hold 'em tournament. While seven-card stud was my game of choice, I had played a lot of Hold 'em. Jim actually preferred Hold 'em, so it was an easy sell to him to make our next excursion a Hold 'em tournament.*

So we headed to the Trop the next month for their weekly no-limit Texas Hold 'em tournament. In a field of about one hundred and fifty players, both my brother-in-law and I made the final table. That was all the encouragement that I needed. After that tournament, I found myself heading to Atlantic City on a regular basis to participate in Hold 'em tournaments.

More important, the experience had a much broader effect on my learning process. I started looking at everything more critically and trying to make connections between different disciplines. I started applying poker strategies to business and vice versa with the former eventually leading to the writing of this book. One constant I find among successful businesspeople is their ability to transform knowledge from one discipline to another. We are presented with clues every day, although we tend to ignore most of them or fail to see their application outside the context in which we view them. There is a world of information out there for those willing to grasp it.

8. POCKET ACES: PLAYING TO WIN

No matter what you are pursuing in your professional and personal life, if it is worthwhile, then it is worth investing the time and effort to make it a success. Success takes time and hard work. The more time and work you put into something, the more you will learn and the better you will become at it. Experience is the best teacher for dealing with the infinite possibilities you potentially face every day.

There are no shortcuts in poker. Even those top players with innate and uncanny abilities cut their teeth on low-stakes games and took their share of losses before being successful. Players may work for years at lower-level games before building up the bankroll and confidence to try higher-stakes games. Even then, they may not succeed, and before too long, they find themselves back at the lower-end tables working to build up their bankroll again.

Success takes time. When you hear of presumed overnight success stories, you are often unaware of the long road of hard work behind that story. In the modern world of televised tournament poker, where each week offers a player the opportunity to become a millionaire, most of the winners are longtime seasoned veterans who have endured their share of failure and trial and error. Yet, occasionally, a relative newcomer will get a rush of cards and break through, but that story is the exception and not the rule.

Life is not a lottery. Yes, luck plays a role in our everyday lives. In a poker tournament with over a thousand entries, it takes a combination of luck and skill to win. Skill alone won't do it. The winner will have to get lucky. And luck alone won't do it, either. You must be skilled and prepared enough to take advantage of those lucky opportunities.

In poker, you never know when an opportunity will present itself. That's why it's so important to be at the ready at all times. You can have two-seven off suit (the worst possible starting hand in poker), but if everyone folds to you on the button, you now have an opportunity. You have position and can use that regardless of your cards. A bad player will fold in that situation and bemoan how unlucky he was that he didn't get any good cards. A good player will raise and steal the blinds there. She uses her skill and cunning to pounce on an opportunity.

You may feel frustrated in your job because the person ahead of you is just as young as you. You can bemoan your unfortunate situation or you can work your hardest. You never know when there will be an opportunity elsewhere in the organization. Or perhaps that person ahead of you will find a new opportunity for advancement—which will create an opportunity for you. You never know. However, if you never give up and keep working hard and getting better, you will be ready to seize an opportunity when it does arise. Become as experienced as you can in your pursuits and you will be successful.

When I started my career working as an attorney on Wall Street, we had a week's worth of orientation. From 9 AM to 5 PM every day, we would go through various exercises and listen to a number of speeches from partners who represented all of the various departments. Of course, we still had our real work to do (after all, law firms only make money from billable hours), so we'd start doing that promptly at 5 PM.

Looking back, I have very few memories of that week, but one thing stood out then and has stuck with me since. One of the partners came in and, speaking in a military tone, stated that our work product had to be perfect. Not only was that expected, he continued, it was the only way they could justify the fees that they charged. No excuses would be tolerated. If you had to miss a few nights' sleep, so be it. Any personal plans had to be flexible. The message could not have been clearer. Our job was to work as hard as we could to put out the best work product possible.

It's a lesson that's always stuck with me. The world's a highly competitive place. If you don't perform, there's a pack of others right behind, ready to take your business, your job, and your money. Nowhere is that more evident than at the poker table. Nine others are seated around the table thinking of ways to separate you from your chips. If I don't work my hardest to make sure that I'm playing the best that I can, I'm going to lose. The competition is easy to see because it's right there. On the job, the competition may not be as visible, but it's there. No one is irreplaceable. In just about every business, people and firms can be replaced. Those who strive for excellence every day will be the ones most likely to maintain their place and replace others.

While a firm grasp of the underlying fundamentals is a necessity in poker, playing by the book will lead to a slow but sure demise. Every player should have a handle on such things as starting-hand requirements, how to play from each position, and pot odds. (There are many excellent beginner poker books that explain these concepts in detail.) This knowledge forms the basis of your thought process at the table. The thought process doesn't end there, however. It begins there. Once you know the hands that you or your opponent should open or raise with from early position, you can begin to strategize. Is your opponent the type of player who plays by the book or will he mix up his play? If he mixes up his play, will he do that in a predictable pattern? Is he capable of making unorthodox moves and does he believe that his opponents are paying close enough attention to make his unorthodox moves worthwhile?

As you try to find answers to these questions regarding each of your opponents, you are trying to make sure that they can't come up with answers about you. You vary your play from the book in order to make your play unpredictable. But are your opponents astute enough to follow? Will they expect you to mix up your play in a certain way—in which case, can you plan for that? Each action you take should have a purpose, and that purpose is to manipulate, control, and lead the actions of your opponents. Since every opponent you face will be different, you must constantly be making adjustments. Even if you're playing against familiar opponents, they will be making adjustments and you will have to make counteradjustments as well.

Poker is the ultimate test of flexibility. Good leaders in any discipline, whether running a company or raising children, must be flexible and adaptable. Yes, we need guidelines and rules, but nothing should be so rigid that there is not enough flexibility built in to adapt to our environment. When we're first starting out, we have to work hard to learn as much as possible about our chosen career. We study in school and learn from peers. At some point, our learning curve should undergo a serious development. We begin to contribute to our own learning curve as we supplement the learning from outside sources.

A good poker player learns to play by the book, makes constant adjustments, and finds the sweet spot through trial and error that suits his style and personality best. He never stops learning and he never stops making adjustments and he never stops making his own discoveries. Every time I play the game, I learn something new. Every business and every career will have those same opportunities.

YOU HAVE FREE WILL—EXERCISE IT

Poker players do not have to chase runners. They do not have to put money in the pot when they have a losing hand. So why do so many players do so? The most common reason is that they allow their cards to dictate their play. They just cannot fold a decent hand even though they know they are beat. A player may start out with a pair of jacks, which is a good starting hand. However, when that player fails to improve, he will stick with the jacks even when his opponent almost certainly has a pair of kings. He just cannot bring himself to fold the hand. He will call three extra bets, knowing he is going to lose. It is almost as if the cards have a magical hold over him.

Of course, objectively, we know that the cards do not possess any such powers. Rather, a critical observer can clearly see that the losing player is a weak player. He feels compelled to call with a losing hand because he lacks objectivity at the moment. Even though he is free to fold that hand, he just cannot bring himself to do it. He mistakenly believes that he has to play these cards because they look so nice. When he inevitably loses, he will still not admit a mistake. I see this happen all the time. A player will play a fair but losing hand all the way to the end, knowing that his opponent is highly likely to have him beat. Then when he loses, the player will announce something like: "Well, I knew you had me beat but I had to call you with the hand I had."

If I was not so happy to have these players at my table, I would scream, "NO, YOU DID NOT HAVE TO PLAY THAT HAND!!!" There is no requirement that you play. You can do anything you want with that hand. Sure, it may have looked nice, but if it is a loser, get rid of it. You have free will. Exercise it.

As obvious a mistake as this may seem at the poker table, we make these mistakes all the time in real life. I know I have bought stock in companies when I was smitten with the concept of what they were doing, even though I knew the fundamentals of the company were shaky. Needless to say, I lost money.

How many times have you made spontaneous purchases that you knew were not good bargains? It is okay to splurge once in a while, but if you find yourself with buyer's remorse more frequently than you would like, remind yourself that you have free will.

How many times have you felt pressured by a pushy salesman into buying something that you really did not want? That suit may look nice on you, but you can put it back on the rack as easily as you can fold those losing jacks. You have free will.

How many times have you felt pressured by a friend or co-worker into doing something that you really did not want to do? You do not have to do it. You have free will. If a fellow employee wants you to do something that is questionable, don't do it.

How many times in your career have you been afraid to speak up because you're not sure how your ideas will be received? The best ideas may meet some initial resistance or be subject to challenge, especially those that are groundbreaking or unorthodox.

I am sure everyone can come up with countless examples of situations where he or she failed to exercise free will. Start taking note of these times and take action to correct it. Free will is one of the greatest gifts we have. When we fail to exercise it, we fail ourselves.

THE FIRST TO ACT USUALLY WINS

In poker, the first person to make a play for the pot usually wins it. By betting out, a player shows strength and puts his opponents on the defensive. The opponents now must make a decision whether to fold, call, or raise. If the first player had not bet, the next opponent's only decision would be whether to bet or check. The opponent would have the luxury of making this decision relatively risk-free, since he knows that the first player did not feel strongly enough about his hand to bet it.

So by betting out first when you have the opportunity, you accomplish two things. First, you send a signal to your opponents that you have a strong hand. Second, your opponents now know that the price of poker just got more expensive. They know it will cost them to stay in the hand, and, furthermore, it is likely that you are in the hand for the long run. Thus, it will cost them a lot of bets to see the hand all the way to the end. By betting first, you increase your chances of winning. You may end up with the best hand and win the pot. Or, by putting your opponents on the defensive, you have an excellent chance of getting them to fold if they are vulnerable. If your opponent calls or raises you, then you have gained some valuable insight into the potential strength of her hand, which may save you money in the long run.

While there is a strategic advantage to betting out at a pot, this is not a tactic to try on every hand. You must pick and choose your spots to employ this tactic. The optimal time to try is when the following conditions exist: there is a good-sized pot worth winning; you have a decent hand but not an overwhelmingly strong hand; and you sense your opponent(s) may be vulnerable. By betting first in this situation, you increase your opportunity to win the pot by putting your opponents on the defensive. Even if you guess wrong and an opponent has a strong hand, the size of the pot makes the play worthwhile. While you may not win this particular pot, if you consistently implement this play at optimal times, overall, you will increase your winnings.

The lesson to be learned here is to be proactive. If a job is up for auction, do your homework and get a bid in. Be the first to act. You have made the first impression, which offers a huge psychological advantage. Your bid shows initiative and drive. If there are other potential bidders out there, you have effectively put them on the defensive. They may even go away in the face of a competing bid. If, on the other hand, they do outbid you, then at least you have gained valuable information that you can now use to make an informed decision as to whether you walk away or make another bid.

BE PREPARED TO EXPLOIT OPPORTUNITIES

Poker can be a very tedious game. The difference between winning and losing often comes down to one hand an hour. That is, the successful player will win on average one extra pot per hour than the average player. Over the long run, that adds up. With up to ten players at a table, opportunities to win are just not that commonplace. Good players are patient and disciplined. They do not play a lot of hands and they are not reckless with their chips. Yet, they are prepared to act at all times. You must be prepared in order to take advantage of an opportunity when it presents itself. There will be times when you do not have a good hand but you are fairly confident your opponent does not either and you can exploit that. Good players stay completely focused on the task at hand so that they do not miss an opportunity. Poker is an unpredictable game, so you never know when you will find the next opportunity to exploit your opponent.

While most pursuits in life are not as random as poker, you still never know when the next opportunity will present itself. The only way to make sure you do not miss an opportunity is to stay completely focused on your quest. I can thank my wife for a great example of applying this concept to our lives. We had been looking to purchase a beach house on the New Jersey Shore and had become increasingly frustrated by the high prices of what was available. I was frustrated to the point of giving up. My wife, however, remained patient and focused. She continued to monitor all of the available listings. During this time, I left for Las Vegas for a prearranged trip. My wife called me when I was in Las Vegas to let me know that a new townhouse just came on the market, and it appeared from its description to be very reasonably priced. I was somewhat skeptical and asked if we could talk about it when I got home. At the time, I was more focused on playing poker.

My wife, to her credit, remained persistent. She set up an appointment for us to see the townhouse that Saturday morning, which was the very first day that the house would be shown. I did not get home until Friday night after a tiring trip that included several late-night poker tournaments. The last thing I felt like doing was getting up before dawn the next morning, packing up, and driving two hours to look at a beach house I thought for sure would be as pricey as the rest we had seen.

Well, the trip was well worth it. The house was perfect and by far the most reasonably priced property we had seen. It seemed too good to be true. We kept looking for the defect. We could not find one. After looking at a few more properties while we were there, we became more convinced that we had really found a great deal. My wife wanted to put in a bid right away. I wanted to wait a day or two so as to not appear overly anxious. Plus, I wanted the time to fully digest the situation. My wife pointed out that this was a rare opportunity and that any hesitation on our part could make us miss out. My wife won out, and we called the seller's agent to make an offer that was slightly below the asking price. The seller accepted our offer, and all that was left to do was sign the papers. However, before we could sign, another prospective buyer put in an offer that was above the asking price. (We insisted on seeing a copy of the other buyer's signed contract offer, which was provided.) The seller came back to us and let us know that if we came up to the asking price, the house was ours. Since we had been the first to act, they wanted to give us the opportunity to buy. (We did not use a separate buyer's agent, and the seller's agent in this case was willing to kick in the difference.) We accepted their deal, and I thanked my wife for making it happen. Her focus found the opportunity and her determination exploited it. If it had been up to me, I would have blown both. Fortunately, my wife was focused and she was able to convince me to get onboard.

As an aside, after we had a signed contract, the other buyer came back with a significantly higher offer, but was too late. This only served to confirm what we already knew—that we had gotten a great deal.

Do Not Chase Runners

In poker terms, chasing runners is when a player who is obviously behind will still call a bet or two, hoping to catch a card that will make his a winning hand. For example, say there are two players remaining in a hand of Hold 'em. The common cards are the ace of hearts, jack of spades, and the two of clubs. Player A is holding ace of spades and jack of clubs, giving him top two pair. Player B is holding the king of clubs and the queen of clubs, giving him a straight draw if he catches a ten and a backdoor flush draw if both of the remaining cards are clubs. But right now all Player B has is a king kicker. He is way behind Player A. If Player A bets aggressively, Player B should fold. However, many loose players will call in that situation even though the odds of their winning are slim. They just cannot resist chasing runners. Once in a while they will catch their cards, which will provide enough encouragement for them to continue the practice. In the long run, however, this is a losing proposition. Even experienced and otherwise strong players will sometimes succumb to the temptation to chase runners—especially when they have not seen any good cards in a while.

Avoid the temptation to chase runners in life. If you are relocating and have spent all day looking at houses to buy, do not make an offer just because you are tired and frustrated. Rather, go home and get a good night's sleep and reevaluate in the morning. There will still be plenty of houses out there.

Before we found our dream beach house, my wife and I narrowly avoided making a big mistake chasing our dream. We had looked at so many houses that were unappealing that we finally made an offer on one that was in good shape but overpriced. Our judgment was clouded from all the houses we had already seen. Most of these houses had been sitting on the market for a while and obviously were not priced to sell. Instead of waiting for the right house to come along, we were chasing runners. In fact, we had a handshake in place. Fortunately for us, the seller got greedy when it came time to sign the contract and he tried to renegotiate the deal. At that point, we walked away. However, if the seller had stuck to the original deal in principle, we would have gone through with the transaction and so missed out on our dream house that came along a few weeks later.

PLAY SMART

Playing smart seems like such a simple concept that it should be the obvious thing to do. In poker, however, it is very easy to forget this concept. Poker is a game, after all. It is very tempting to play hands just for fun, even when you know it is not smart to play. It is easy to let your opponent off the hook when you could have squeezed an extra bet out of him. It sometimes feels that it is not worth the effort to study and observe your opponent. It can, at times, be boring to play in a disciplined way. In short, sometimes you just do not want to play smart. You just want to play.

Successful poker players work hard at poker. Their enjoyment comes from executing their hands properly and winning. Even if these players lose a hand, they do not get discouraged as long as they played correctly. They understand the fundamentals and consistently apply them. They grind out their wins over the long term by continuing to play smart and disciplined. For them, poker is a skill that they pursue with all due earnestness.

There are times, however, when poker should just be a game. For the recreational player, or even the professional player who at times just wants to blow off steam, poker should be fun. If you have that urge, then play a low-stakes game with money set aside purely for recreational purposes.

All of us work hard throughout our lives. We work hard at our jobs, raising our children, and taking care of our homes. If we consistently work smart at these pursuits, we will hopefully have successful careers, well-adjusted children, and clean, comfortable homes. To reach these results requires our understanding and executing the fundamentals on a consistent basis. We cannot decide not to be a parent because it is tiring. We can, however, take time out from the daily grind to just have fun. As much intrinsic value as we receive from playing smart in our daily pursuits, it is important to remember that life can be a game, too. Have fun with it and blow off steam. It will help refresh you and allow you to continue to play smart in the long run.

YOU CAN'T BLUFF A SUCKER

This maxim is well understood in the poker community but difficult for nonplayers to understand. They find it counterintuitive. Isn't a sucker easy to bluff? Isn't that what makes him a sucker? Surprisingly, the answer is no. In poker, bluffs are used only on rare occasions and typically only against better players. There are some weak players who will fold to any bet unless they have a really strong hand. Certainly, these players can be dominated, and experienced players will consistently bet into them.

A true sucker, however, wants action. This is the player that will bet, raise, and call with any hand. He finds it empowering to throw chips around. He finds it emasculating to fold a hand, no matter how weak it is. He is recklessly optimistic about every hand. He will win his fair share of hands, since he is playing them all, but will bleed money overall. Those wins will give him a false sense of success and will reinforce his self-destructive play.

It is pointless to try to bluff such a player. Good players will not try. Rather, a good player will wait until he knows he has a better hand than the sucker and then bet, bet, bet. The sucker is sure to call or even raise and pay off the good player. A sucker wants to give his money away so there is no reason to take chances with him. Wait until you have the better hand and then take his money.

Avoid being a sucker in your everyday life. Do you need to buy every latest gadget? Do you find yourself trading in your car every other year for a new one? Do you buy things you do not need just because they are on sale? If you need constant action, find inexpensive hobbies.

Take an honest assessment of your work relationships. Are you a team player surrounded by individuals? Do people ask for your assistance but refuse to give you credit? Are you doing the work of others at the expense of your own? If you want to get ahead, it's certainly a good idea to go above and beyond the call of duty and help out your co-workers. Just make sure you get some of the recognition as well.

While no one likes to consider himself a sucker, most of us engage in some level of self-destructive behavior in some aspect of our lives. To correct such behavior requires an honest self-assessment. Take inventory of your life to weed out any self-destructive behavior. Don't be a sucker in the poker game of life.

STAND UP FOR YOURSELF

Poker is the ultimate "solo" game where you play against others. There are no teammates. No one has your back. You and only you are responsible for your play. Win or lose, you must take all of the credit or all of the blame. Additionally, unlike other solo games, such as chess, you have more than one opponent. Depending on what game of poker you are playing, you can have up to nine other opponents at the table. If you are playing a tournament, you can have hundreds of other opponents. In such an environment, you truly must have a "me against the world" mentality. If you do not stand up for yourself, no one else will.

Standing up for yourself does not mean bullying other people. It means sticking up for your rights, defending yourself against the actions of others and, if the situation calls for it, competing to succeed. No matter what the situation, always assume going in that you are doing it alone. Learn not to rely or depend on anyone or anything outside of yourself. Become totally self-sufficient. Adopt a "me against the world" attitude. Then if you do receive outside assistance, you will be that much better off.

When you receive a new project at work, however, you may find the need to consult others. If that's the case, then seek that advice immediately, as you never know how limited their availability may be. In any event, take inventory up front of everything that needs to be done, then prioritize any aspect that may require outside assistance. As the deadline approaches, you don't want to have to rely on anyone but yourself.

LEARN FROM THE MISTAKES OF OTHERS

The good player studies the play of his opponents. He does this for several reasons. First and foremost, he wants to get a read on his opponent's playing style and betting patterns in order to gain an edge in how he plays each opponent. Next, the good player wants to be on the alert to see how his opponents react to every situation. Do they go on tilt easily? Do they lose their cool? Can they be goaded into making bad plays? Finally, one of the most overlooked reasons for studying opponents is to learn from their mistakes. The good player knows he can learn as much from an opponent's mistake (especially a good opponent) as he can from his own. Just as the potential situations in poker are endless, the mistakes that can be made are infinite as well. You will never live long enough to make all of them yourself. To become as experienced as you can, you must learn from the mistakes of others. If you are playing in a controlling manner, you may play only 10 to 20 percent of the hands dealt. Nonetheless, if you are not paying attention to those other hands, you are wasting your time. You are not learning from the great majority of hands that you are dealt.

Every day is an opportunity to learn. You can learn a lot from people you come in contact with every day. Even if we are not participating in any major (or minor) decisions on a particular day, we are likely to interact with friends and co-workers. Take an interest in their lives. Ask questions of them. Between all of them, at least one of them is likely to have something going on that will be of interest to you at a later time.

Find a mentor or two at work. Ask questions and soak up as much information as you can. Use your mentor as a sounding board for ideas you may have. Keep in touch with former classmates and co-workers. They will likely be confronting many of the same issues you face, since they will be of similar age and share many goals and interests. They can prove invaluable in providing advice and may even present you with some new opportunities.

Do Not Waste Time Worrying about Things that You Cannot Control

In order to remain emotionally detached, players must distinguish between those things that are within their control and those that are not. Players can control their own play. They can be vigilant at the table so they can properly analyze the situation and make the best decision at that time based on the information available to them. Players cannot control luck or their opponents, though they can influence them. When good players suffer a bad beat, they put it behind them and keep playing their game.

Do not worry about the things that you cannot control in your life. Rather, prepare for them and learn to deal with them. Be diversified in your investments to minimize risk. Be adequately insured for every potential liability. Maintain sufficient liquid assets in the event of an emergency. Live below your means.

When you do suffer a setback, take the time to analyze what happened. If the setback happened due to something you could have controlled, take steps to correct it. If the setback happened due to forces outside of your control, put it behind you and do not let it affect your future decisions.

A Good Player Can Be Bluffed

A good player can be bluffed. This is perhaps the biggest paradox in all of poker. Aren't the great players able to sniff out every bluff? Isn't this what separates the winners from the losers? Don't the great ones look a bluffer straight in the eye, see into his soul, and call the bluff without flinching?

Certainly, the hallmark of a great player is her ability to read her opponents. Even when she cannot get a good read on her opponent, she will fight back rather than let her opponent run all over her. However, there are plenty of times when a good player can be bluffed. The reason is quite simple. The good player knows not to act when she cannot perceive an advantage. She will not waste her money when her opponent has the advantage. Why call an opponent who may or may not be bluffing when you can save your money to put to use when you know you have an advantage? The bottom line is that the good player will not take someone else's bet when she does not have an edge. Rather, she will save her money to bet when she has the upper hand.

Play to your own strengths in your life. Do not play someone else's strong hand. Everyone loves to offer advice on everything from stocks to restaurants. Take all of the advice with a grain of salt. Be discriminating. Certainly, more caution should be taken with a stock tip as opposed to the restaurant recommendation. Still, do you want to waste money and a precious night out on a lousy restaurant? Go where you want to go, not where someone else talks you into going. Live your life the way you want to, not according to someone else's direction. You do not have to keep up with the Joneses or the Smiths or anyone else. You only have to please yourself and your loved ones.

Everyone has his own unique perspective on life. Each of us has our own particular likes and dislikes. We all have varying degrees of risk tolerance. Our wants, ambitions, and desires differ from person to person. It is fine to share tips, advice, and recommendations within our inner circles. It is equally worthwhile to listen to the advice of experts in a given field. We can all learn from the experiences of others. At the end of the day, however, we have to live our own lives within our own comfort zone. Learn to make the decisions that are right for you. Be proactive. Act when you have an advantage. Play into your own strengths, not into your neighbor's strengths.

Life is full of options. Wait for one to your liking. Be discriminating. Spend your time and resources on the option that is best suited for you.

A LIFETIME OF DECISIONS

Throughout these pages, I've repeatedly emphasized how success in poker is measured over the long term. By concentrating on making correct decisions on a consistent basis, success will follow despite short-term setbacks. Of course, no matter how proficient someone is in poker, he will make mistakes. No one is perfect, and to compound matters, poker is a game of imperfect information. Players must rely on their experience and perceptive abilities to take the course of action they believe is correct at the time. They will not always be right. Expert players will make mistakes big and small. Additionally, those same players will make correct decisions that won't work out as envisioned due to the arbitrary and capricious nature of playing cards. In the long run, those players will succeed because they have the will, determination, and foresight to steer through the mistakes and bad luck and make a lot more right answers than wrong ones.

We'll all face a lifetime of decisions big and small. We'll all make some small mistakes and some big ones. The real world can be chaotic and cruel. It can deal your opponent a one outer on the river and crush your aspirations. All we can do is rely on our experience and intuition to make correct decisions at the time we face them. We won't always be right, but, again, with will, determination, foresight, and grit we can make correct decisions consistently enough to enjoy a lifetime of success and happiness.

WHEN IN DOUBT, PLAY

There are times in poker when you just do not know if it is beneficial to play a hand. No matter what your level of experience or knowledge, you will face hands that will be difficult for you to determine whether or not you should play them. In those situations, my advice is to play. You only live once. So, when in doubt, play. If you lose, learn from the experience. If you win, so much the better. At least you will not have doubts.

There will be plenty of decisions in life that are a flip of the coin. There will be all kinds of decisions from the little ones, like whether to go out to dinner, to the big ones, such as whether to buy a new home. If you have doubts, then by all means decline or postpone—especially with the big decisions. But if you are truly on the fence and are genuinely undecided, then you may want to play. You only live once. Be a player in life, not just an observer.

THE POKER EXPERIENCE

Playing with Legends

I have been playing poker on a regular basis for over twenty-five years. During most of that time, I was strictly a recreational player. I played with the utmost seriousness and I played to win, but I played as a hobby. I enjoyed the competitive atmosphere and the challenge of trying to win and better my play.

It wasn't until the late 1990s that I started to play tournament poker. I found tournament poker more to my liking because you have a way of measuring your success every time out. Even if you are playing tournament poker, success should be measured over the long term—more than a few tournaments. However, I find it easier to learn from my mistakes in tournaments because they get magnified. Make a mistake in a cash game and you lose a pot. If you end the session ahead, it's likely you won't spend much time thinking about that mistake that cost you a pot. Make a mistake in a tournament and it often means elimination. You are forced to acknowledge, recognize, and learn from those mistakes.

In the years before the poker boom, the Tropicana, as noted earlier, was the only casino in Atlantic City that had daily poker tournaments. I would try to play a few Hold 'em events each year. Once a year, the US Poker Championships would come to the Trump Taj Mahal in Atlantic City. At the time, that was the only major tourna-

ment to come to Atlantic City and one of only a handful held anywhere throughout the year. I always looked forward to that time of year and I would try to play one or two of the lower-priced events of the US Poker Championships.

My larger poker ambitions at the time were to play a few big-entry events including—at some point in my life—the main event of the World Series of Poker. I was not in a real hurry and figured I would never play such a large event unless I won my way in through a satellite. I had, and still have, a successful career as a corporate lawyer, and poker was a great way to relieve stress. I have always found many similarities between poker and business, so it was also a good way to keep fresh and find new perspectives for both disciplines.

In 2003, everything changed. Three critical events converged to start a poker revolution. First, online poker sites popped up like virtual mushrooms overnight, affording anyone with a computer the opportunity to play anytime with a few clicks of the mouse. No longer did you need to live within driving distance of a casino to gain experience. Next, the World Poker Tour made its debut on the Travel Channel, and the exciting coverage made poker an overnight television success. Finally, the aptly named Chris Moneymaker won the main event of the World Series of Poker that year after qualifying by spending $40 on an online satellite. The victory of this underdog gave hope to millions throughout the world.

For me, 2003 was also a changing point in my poker career. I had been playing more and more tournaments and enjoying greater success. At the time, there was not much literature on the subject. Poker and writing were my biggest hobbies. As much as I had combined poker strategies with other disciplines and vice versa, it had never occurred to me to merge my poker and writing. I felt strongly that I had some unique perspectives on poker that would be beneficial to many players. I wrote my first poker book that year (Tournament Poker and the Art of War).

As the poker boom continued, I found myself playing in more and bigger events. I also tapped into a wealth of information I had been storing up to complete some more books on poker strategy. This book is the one that I wanted most of all to write, for it embodies so much of what I have learned in poker and business over the last twenty-five years.

My poker ambitions have changed over time. Whereas a few years ago my dreams were to play in a high-profile event, I have now already played in some of the most prestigious events and have made the televised table a number of times. I was fortunate to receive an invitation to play in a couple of events in the very first year of the Professional Poker Tour (PPT). The PPT is a series of no-limit Texas Hold 'em tournaments limited to the top players who must qualify to participate.

During these events, I found myself playing side by side such legends as Doyle Brunson and T. J. Cloutier—men whose books I read many years ago when I was really trying to learn the game. I was going heads-up in pots with World Poker Tour champions and World Series of Poker bracelet winners. It was a thrill and a challenge, but I never found it intimidating. Much like my first game that rainy night down the Jersey Shore, I found it exhilarating.

I played my first event in the PPT clear across the country in San Jose, California, at the Bay 101 Casino. I came in twentieth place out over two hundred of the best players in the world. In a poker tournament, though, there is only one place that you want to finish, and it's not twentieth. When I got knocked out, it was a huge letdown, even though I thought I had played well for the better part of two days. There would be no rides on the boardwalk that night. Rather, I called my wife to tell her I loved her and to say good-night. Then I went to bed thinking of the next challenge.

GLOSSARY

Below is a list of common poker terms. Not all are used in this book, but each will be helpful if you ever venture into a poker room.

Ace rag: In Hold 'em, to have an ace and a card below a ten.

All-in: To place all of one's chips in the pot. To go "all-in" is to bet your entire stack.

Ante: A set amount of chips that each player (including the blinds) must place in the pot before a hand is dealt. In no-limit Hold 'em tournaments, antes typically are not required until the later rounds.

Bad beat: Having a strong hand beaten by an opponent who was an underdog who made a lucky draw. This is especially true when your opponent is playing poorly and should not have been in the pot in the first place.

Best of it: Having the best chance of winning the hand at that particular time.

Bet: To be the first to place chips in the pot on any given round.

Big blind: Typically the position that is two spots to the left of the button. The big blind must lead the first round of betting with a forced full bet.

Blank: A card that does not help any player.

Blind: A forced bet that one or two players make to start the first round of betting. The blinds will be the first to act in each subsequent round of betting, and, thus, to be in the blind is to be in an unfavorable position. The blinds rotate around the table with each deal and are always to the left of the button.

Blinded out: To lose your chip stack as a result of posting the mandatory blinds and antes.

Bluff: A bet or raise made to force your opponent to fold when you sense he is vulnerable, even though he may have a better hand.

Board: The five community cards placed in the center of the table in Texas Hold 'em.

Button: A round disc that rotates around the table with each new deal. The player on the button acts last during each round of betting, and, thus, to be on the button is to be in the most favorable position.

Buy information: Calling a bet when you are pretty sure you do not have the best hand but you want to find out what cards your opponent is playing.

Call: To place in the pot an amount of chips equal to an opponent's bet or raise.

Caller: A player who makes a call.

Calling station: A weak player who will call just about any bet but will rarely bet or raise. This type of player is extremely hard to bluff.

Chase: To stay in a hand with hopes of outdrawing an opponent with a superior hand.

Check: To pass when it is your turn to bet.

Check-raise: To check and then raise after your opponent bets.

Chip: A round token used to represent varying denominations of money.

Come over the top: To raise or re-raise with a huge bet.

Community cards: The five cards making the board that are dealt face up in the center of the table and are shared by all of the players.

Covered: To have someone covered means you have more chips than he does.

Drawing dead: Holding a hand that cannot possibly win because no matter what card comes up, your opponent will still hold a superior hand.

Draw out: To improve your hand so that it beats a previous superior hand.

Early position: Any position in which you will act before most of the other players in a round of betting. In a ten-handed game, the first five positions to the left of the button will be considered early positions.

Favorite: A hand that has the best chance of winning, at any point in time, before all of the cards are dealt.

Fifth street: The fifth and final community card in Hold 'em or the sixth card dealt in seven-card stud. Also called the river in Hold 'em.

Flop: The first three community cards, which are all dealt at the same time.

Flush: Five cards of the same suit.

Fold: To drop out of a hand rather than call a bet or raise.

Fourth street: The fourth community card in Hold 'em or the fourth card dealt in seven-card stud. Also called the *turn* in Hold 'em.

Free card: A card that a player gets to see without having to pay for it. When no one bets on a particular round of playing, the next card is considered a free card.

Freeroll: A tournament that is free to enter for each of the players.

Freezeout: A standard tournament structure where play continues until every player is eliminated but one.

Full house: Three cards of one rank and two of another such as king, king, king, three, three.

Gut shot: An inside straight draw.

Heads-up: To play against a single opponent.

In the money: In tournament play, only the top finishers will receive prize money. A player who advances to receive prize money is said to have finished in the money.

Inside straight draw: A straight that can be completed only by a card of one rank. For example, three-four-five-seven can only be completed with a six.

Kicker: A side card that is not part of any made hand.

Late position: Any position in which you will act after most of the other players in a round of betting. In a ten-handed game, the button and the two positions to the right of the button will be considered late positions.

Laydown: To fold your hand in the face of a bet.

Levels: Predetermined intervals of play whereby the blinds (and antes, if applicable) will be set for a period of time. The blinds will increase with each level.

Limp in: To call a bet rather than raise prior to the flop.

Loose: A player who is playing loose is playing more hands than he should.

Middle pair: To pair the second-highest card on the board.

Middle position: A position in a round of betting somewhere in the middle. In a ten-handed game, the fourth and fifth position to the right of the button are considered middle positions.

Muck: To discard a hand without revealing it.

Multiway hand or pot: A hand or pot with three or more players.

Nuts: The best possible hand at that point in time.

Off suit: Two or more cards of different suits. If you are dealt the jack of diamonds and the ten of spades, your hand is jack ten off suit.

On the bubble: In tournament play, when players are only a few eliminations away from being in the money. If a player is eliminated in twenty-eighth place when twenty-seven places are paid, that player is said to have been eliminated on the bubble.

On tilt: To be playing poorly due to a lack of control of your own play.

Open-ended straight draw: Four cards to a straight, which can be completed by cards of two different ranks. Seven-eight-nine-ten is an open-ended straight draw in that either a jack or six will complete the straight.

Outs: When you do not have the best hand but there are still more cards to come, those cards that will make your hand a winning hand are called your outs.

Over card(s): To have a card(s) that is higher than any card on the board. If you have king, jack and the flop is queen, four, seven, then you have one over card.

Pair: Two cards of the same rank such as six, six.

Pot: The collective amount of all chips bet at any point in time.

Pot odds: The ratio of the number of chips in the pot to the size of the bet you must call.

Put someone on a hand: To determine to the best of your ability the hand your opponent is most likely to possess.

Rainbow: Two to four cards of different suits. If the flop comes three, six, jack rainbow, then there are not two cards of any one suit.

Raise: To bet an additional amount after an opponent makes a bet.

Raiser: A player who makes a raise.

Ring game: A single-table nontournament game of poker. Also called a side game.

River: The fifth and final community card in Hold 'em.

Runner: A card that helps or completes your hand when you need help and that comes on the turn and/or river. For example, you are holding jack of hearts, ten of hearts and the flop is jack of spades, ace of hearts, two of diamonds. Your opponent is holding ace of diamonds, jack of clubs. Since no one card will help you, you need two runners in order to win. If the turn is four of hearts and the river is nine of hearts, you will have hit two runners and made a flush to win the hand.

Semi-bluff: To bet with the intention of inducing an opponent with a superior hand to fold, but if he does not, you have a reasonable chance to improve your hand to the best hand.

Set: In Hold 'em, three of a kind when you have a pocket pair and the board contains a card of the same rank.

Short-stacked: Playing with a stack of chips that is much smaller than the average chip stack of the other players.

Showdown: The turning over of all remaining players' cards after the last round of betting is concluded.

Side game: A single-table nontournament game of poker. Also called a ring game.

Sixth street: The sixth card dealt in seven-card stud.

Slow play: To not bet or raise with a strong hand in order to trap your opponent and, ultimately, win more chips in the hand.

Steal: To make a big bet or raise that induces your opponent(s) to fold when you may not have the best hand.

Straight: Five cards of mixed suits in sequence.

Suited: Two or more cards of the same suit.

Tell: A nuance or mannerism a player may display that subconsciously gives away his hand.

Tight: Playing very conservatively or only playing strong hands.

Tilt: When a player's emotions get the best of her and clouds her judgment, she is on tilt.

Underdog: A hand that is not the favorite to win.

Under the gun: The first player to act on the first round of betting in Hold 'em. Since the blinds have forced bets, the player to the immediate left of the big blind is under the gun.

Worst of it: Being an underdog to your opponent(s) at that point in time.

A POKER PRIMER

TEXAS HOLD 'EM BASICS

Texas Hold 'em (or just plain Hold 'em) is poker's hottest game and it can be played either as a limit game or a no-limit game. Hold 'em is a seven-card flop game represented by two cards unique to each player and five community cards that are shared by everyone. Each player then makes his best five-card hand. To begin, each player is dealt two cards face down. These are the player's hole cards or down cards and can only be seen by the player holding the cards. The cards are dealt clockwise beginning with the player to the "dealer's" immediate left. The dealer is represented by a small white disc called the button. With each passing hand, the button is passed to the player to the left. While the casino dealer never changes seats, he deals the cards based on where the button is located.

The first player to the left of the button is called the small blind. The second player to the left of the button is called the big blind. Together, they are called the blinds. The players in the blinds must post bets before the cards are dealt. The big blind must put in one full bet, and the small blind typically puts in one-half of a full bet. For instance, in a $20 to $40 limit Hold 'em game, a full bet for the first round is $20. The big blind posts the $20 bet, and the small blind must post a half bet of $10. Since the blinds have already posted their bets, the action begins with the player to the immediate left of the big blind once the cards have been dealt. This player now has the option of calling (matching the full bet amount of the big blind), raising, or folding. In limit play, the player can raise only one full bet, which would be $20 in addition to the original $20 for $40 total. In no-limit play, the player can raise any amount from $20 to his entire stack. This first player to act is referred to as being under the gun, since he must make a decision before knowing what any other player will do.

After the first player acts, the action then continues clockwise around the table. Each player has the option of calling, raising, or folding. In limit play, there is typically a limit to how many total raises there can be in any round of betting. For instance, if there are only three total raises, the action would be capped at $80 (i.e., the original $20 bet and three additional $20 raises). In no-limit, just as the name suggests, there is no limit to the number of raises nor how much one can raise.

When the action gets to the blinds, they have a couple of choices. The small blind is already in for a one-half bet. So if no one has raised, the small blind only has to put in another one-half bet in order to call. Of course, the small blind can raise or fold as well. Depending on what has transpired before the action gets to the big blind, he has a couple of choices. First, if no one has raised the big blind, he can check, since he has already posted a full bet. If he checks, he gets to continue playing without spending any more money. The big blind also has the option of raising. Since the big blind had to post his initial bet without the benefit of seeing his cards, he has the option of raising once he has seen his cards.

Once the first round of betting is complete, the dealer will "burn" one card (the top card on the deck does not play) and then lay three cards face up in the center of the table. These three cards are turned over simultaneously and are collectively referred to as the flop. Everyone at the table can use these community cards. The betting starts anew with the first player to the left of the dealer, who is still required to act first. This person can either check or bet. To check means to decline the opportunity to make a bet. He does this by either saying, "Check," or by tapping the table with his hand. If he checks, it does not mean he is out of the hand. He should not throw his cards away when he checks. Even if he does not like his cards, he should hold onto them until everyone has had a chance to act. If everyone still in the hand checks as well, then he will get to see the next card for free. That is, he will not have to post any more money. However, once he checks, the action will move to the next person going clockwise. That person will now have the same opportunity to check or bet. But as soon as anybody bets, the players who act after the bettor cannot check—they must either fold, call, or raise. Those players who checked before the bettor will also be required to either fold, call, or raise, as the action will now continue around. Before we get to the next card, everyone still in the hand must have put in an equal amount of money. The sole exception is when someone is all-in. That means that that player has all of her chips in the pot, in which case she is only eligible to win that portion of the pot that matches her contribution.

Once this second round of betting is over, the dealer will burn another card before turning over one more community card face up adjacent to the flop cards. This card is called the turn card or fourth street. Each player now has six cards from which to make his or her best five-card hand. The betting proceeds exactly as in the second round. In limit play, the betting amounts typically double on this round. For instance, if you are playing $20 to $40 limit Hold 'em, the betting increments for the first two rounds are $20. In the third and fourth round of betting, the betting increments double to $40. In no-limit, any opening bet must be at least equal to the amount of the big blind, no matter what round you are in. Of course, a player can bet or raise up to his entire stack at any time.

After the third round of betting is complete, the dealer will burn one more card and turn over one last community card. This card is called the river or fifth street. Now everyone has seven cards (the five shared community cards and each player's unique two hole cards) from which to make the best five-card hand. Players can use any five-card combination of these seven cards to make a hand. The betting sequence is exactly the same as rounds two and three. Now, after this round of betting is complete, we come to the showdown. Each player remaining in the hand will reveal his cards, and the best hand will win all of the money in the pot. If at any point before the showdown one player makes a bet or raise and no one else calls, then that player wins the pot without a showdown. This can happen in any round of betting from before the flop to fifth street.

HAND RANKINGS

The following are the ranks of poker hands starting with the best. Keep in mind that poker is a five-card game, so you always use the five cards that make your best hand. Other than the royal flush, the ranks of the card are examples; other cards could make up the same hand.

Name	Example
Royal flush	Ace-king-queen-jack-ten (all of the same suit).
Straight flush	Seven-six-five-four-three (all of the same suit). In the event of a tie, the straight flush with the highest-ranking card wins.
Four of a kind	Two-two-two-two-jack. In the event of a tie, the highest four of a kind wins (i.e., four kings beats four jacks).
Full house	Queen-queen-queen-four-four. In the event of a tie, highest rank of the three of a kind wins (i.e., a hand made up of three queens and two fours beats a hand made up of three jacks and two tens).

Flush	King-queen-eight-five-two (all of the same suit). In the event of a tie, the highest ranked card wins (i.e., a king-high flush beats a jack-high flush).
Straight	Nine-eight-seven-six-five (not all of the same suit). In the event of a tie, the straight to the highest-ranking card wins.
Three of a kind	Five-five-five-queen-jack. In the event of a tie, the highest-ranking three of a kind wins (i.e., three sevens beats three fives).
Two pair	King-king-seven-seven-ace. In the event of a tie, the highest-ranking top pair wins (i.e., ace-ace-two-two beats king-king-queen-queen).
One pair	Queen-queen-ace-six-five.
No pair	King-jack-eight-six-two.

Kickers are used to break ties. For instance, ace-ace-four-four-ten would beat ace-ace-four-four-six. The former hand has a ten kicker, which would beat the latter hand's six kicker. Kickers are never used beyond five cards, however. For example, say the final board in Texas Hold 'em looked like this: nine-eight-seven-six-five. Player A is holding ace-ace, and Player B is holding five-six. Since the best five cards either could use is the straight on the board, the players' hole cards would not play and they would split the pot.

ABOUT THE AUTHOR

David Apostolico has been playing poker for more than twenty-five years and is one of the foremost authorities on the subject. His previous books include *Tournament Poker and the Art of War*, *Machiavellian Poker Strategy*, *Lessons from the Pro Poker Tour*, and *Lessons from the Felt*. David also writes, or has written, for the following publications: *Card Player* magazine, *Poker Pro* magazine, *Top Pair*, and pokerpages.com.

David received his JD, with honors, from the University of North Carolina School of Law in 1988. Upon graduation, David went to work for the Wall Street law firm of Winthrop, Stimson, Putnam & Roberts, where he spent a number of years specializing in mergers and acquisitions. During his legal career in both private practice and inhouse at a large corporation, David has found the principles he has learned at the poker table to be enormously useful in his negotiations on behalf of clients large and small, from multibillion dollar corporations to family businesses. David sits on the board of directors of a number of corporations.

David lives with his wife and three sons outside of Philadelphia and plays competitive poker whenever he gets the opportunity.